"In language that is poetic yet unadorned, it's part memoir, part manifesto, part philosophical discourse and wholly enjoyable."
—*San Francisco Chronicle*

David Mas Masumoto

AUTHOR of *EPITAPH FOR A PEACH*

HARVESTING LEGACIES FROM THE LAND

Wisdom of the Last Farmer

FOREWORD BY DAN BARBER
Executive Chef and Co-owner of Blue Hill Farm

Also by David Mas Masumoto

Heirlooms: Letters from a Peach Farmer (2007)

Letters to the Valley: A Harvest of Memories (2004)

Four Seasons in Five Senses: Things Worth Savoring (2003)

Harvest Son: Planting Roots in American Soil (1998)

Epitaph for a Peach: Four Seasons on My Family Farm (1995)

Wisdom of the Last Farmer

Harvesting Legacies from the Land

David Mas Masumoto

Free Press
New York London Toronto Sydney

Free Press
A Division of Simon & Schuster, Inc.
1230 Avenue of the Americas
New York, NY 10020

First Free Press trade paperback edition June 2010

Designed by Ellen R. Sasahara

Manufactured in the United States of America

1 3 5 7 9 10 8 6 4 2

The Library of Congress has cataloged the hardcover edition as follows:

Masumoto, David Mas.
Wisdom of the last farmer : harvesting legacies from the land / David Mas Masumoto.—1st ed.
p. cm.
1. Masumoto, David Mas. 2. Peach growers—California—Biography. 3. Organic farmers—California—Biography. 4. Farm life—California. I. Title. II. Title: Harvesting legacies from the land.
S417.M366A3 2009
630.92—dc22
[B] 2009008229

ISBN 978-1-4165-9930-2
ISBN 978-1-4391-8242-0 (pbk)
ISBN 978-1-4391-1758-3 (ebook)

Dedicated to my father

Contents

Part Four ❧ *Planting Memories*

Part Five ❧ *Succession*

Foreword

I FIRST HEARD OF Mas in 1994, when I was in the kitchen at Chez Panisse and a dessert leaving the pastry station caught my eye. Actually I more or less gasped in disbelief, and that's not because the dessert was so beautiful or ornate (it was) or because I hadn't seen a dessert like it before (I hadn't). I gasped because it was so *crazy.* It was a single peach on a dessert plate, no sprig of mint, no swish of raspberry sauce. It was Peach, unadorned.

I walked my New York City attitude over to the pastry chefs and began to laugh. The peaches were stacked on the counter, delicately wrapped in cellophane and lined up like soldiers, awaiting gastronomic deployment. The chefs lovingly cradled each peach on its way to the plate; the waiters dutifully ferried them away, walking gingerly as though they were carrying soufflés.

"Wow, tough night," I said to the pastry chef. She looked at me but did not respond. So I picked up a dessert menu and was introduced to my first California farmer. "Mas Masumoto, Sun Crest Peach" it said, and nothing more.

Back then chefs didn't name farmers; *organic* or *local* weren't buzzwords on restaurant menus. The sign of a serious restaurant was to present impossibly large imported raspberries in the middle of January. Your average diner still thought *foodshed* meant some kind of food storage; *greening* was about making lots of money.

These days restaurant menus spell it all out, boasting of not just connections to farmers but also of farming methods and philosophies: the volume's been turned up on food consciousness and awareness, and while that's a good thing for chefs and farmers and eaters everywhere, sometimes it gets a little deafening.

You won't find that kind of fanfare on the menu at Chez Panisse. The food continues to be described with plain language and a kind of painstaking honesty. Which suits Alice Waters just fine because she's exacting and disciplined, but even more so because she has farmers like Mas Masumoto supplying the restaurant. All *they* need to announce themselves is their product.

I'd like to say when I finally took a bite of a peach later that night the lights dimmed and the warmth of a religious spirit came over me. The truth is a little less poetic: when I smelled that peach, I thought I'd never smelled something so peachy.

I bit into it and the fruit melted. I was struck by the acidity as much as the sweetness, like a nicely balanced wine. The juice ran down my face and chin. One bite, and then another few bites, and pretty soon all that remained were bits of flesh sticking to my face.

It was the best peach of my life; but I have to qualify that because, like most Americans born in the last fifty years, I didn't know what a peach should taste like. Breeders in the '70s and '80s created low-acid, high-sugar peaches that can be picked when they're still hard, making them suitable for withstanding the rigors of cross-country travel. So we got drunk on sugar, and created taste memories that are more Mrs. Butterworth than Mother Nature. We fell for the wrong woman, and we're still paying for it.

But my greatest memory from that night is the reaction those peaches got from the older diners. Waiters reported several tables saying the same thing: "I haven't had a peach like that since I was a child!" The diners tore apart the peaches with their hands, talking happily about summer afternoons in their grandmother's backyard, lazy mornings in the hammock, the smell of a late August evening.

They were incredible peaches, no doubt. But more than that—as if a peach needs to be more than that—they did that night what I suspect Mas is most thrilled about.

They got people to consider the connection between good food, which is of course food grown in the right way and picked at the most perfect moment, and the memorable moments of life.

And that's the feeling you get when you read this book. *Wis-*

dom of the Last Farmer is about more than farming a great peach. It's about a family that's been shaped by the land over three generations. It's about a father and his son. It's about wisdom and humanity, and homegrown memories, the way a great taste—a meaningful one—has its own kind of DNA. There's nothing in the world more delicious than that.

—Dan Barber
Executive chef and
co-owner of Blue Hill Farm

Part One

Why Farm?

Chapter One

FAMILY HEIRLOOM

I DRIVE TO OUR farmyard on a tractor, dragging a plow that broke when I hooked a vine. I had been working too fast, trying to keep pace with the warm spring days and early rains and the ensuing assault of weeds. My dad works behind the shed, wandering around his tractor.

It's February and our eighty-acre organic farm in California explodes with life. Peaches and nectarines are blooming, and grapevines are pushing out pale green buds with miniature bunches of grapes. In three months, if all goes well, we will gorge ourselves on the first peaches of the season. In six months, we can dry the bulbous grapes into raisins.

But the weeds are flourishing, too. Innocent-looking for a day or so, they keep growing, spreading thick over the landscape until, soon, a lush, tangled mass of fibers competes for water, nutrients, and sunlight, stunting the development of my crops, robbing fruits of the essentials they need to grow fat.

I am an organic farmer of peaches, nectarines, and grapes in Central Valley, California. Organic farming is not simple or easy, and the physical work breaks me. Everyone tells my father and me that it's too hard to farm organically and survive financially, to make money at it. It's easy to want to be environmentally responsible, but it's a damned hard thing to achieve. I cannot replace tedious labor with faster technology or equipment when things go wrong.

My father and I do most of the work ourselves. With our budget getting tighter and tighter every year, our farm demands more and more hard labor. It's exhausting. If we miss a few worms when they appear on leaves or on young fruit, a ruinous outbreak can ensue that we can't fix with a fast-killing chemical spray. An infestation is like catching a bad flu with no medicine readily available. I often whisper to myself, "This farm is going to kill me." So, this week, I have asked my seventy-six-year-old father to do some extra disking for me—to help cultivate and plow under the weeds. For a moment, I believe I might catch up.

Dad shuffles around his tractor as the engine roars. He looks perplexed. At first I wonder if he's trying to listen for something wrong with the engine.

Dad is great at repairs. He had to be, since our family was poor. My grandparents emigrated from Japan a hundred years ago with dreams of owning a farm. Instead, they found racist alien land laws that prevented foreign-born "Orientals" from buying property. So they worked and waited, expecting that their American-born children would be able to purchase land and establish a farm, but World War II intervened and they were all relocated to internment camps, together with all Japanese Americans from the West Coast. Because they looked like the enemy, our family spent four years behind barbed wire in the Arizona desert. Afterward, with no other place to go, they wandered back to Fresno, California. In 1950, after more years of field work, Dad finally realized his own father's dream and was able to buy our farm.

Like most farms in the area, we started with grapes for drying into raisins, muscats for cheap wine, and stone fruits—plums, peaches, and nectarines. Eventually we gravitated into mostly peaches and grapes because they worked well in our soil, and we loved to eat them, especially the rejects that grew too soft to sell.

Isolated and without capital, Dad quickly learned how to restore and repair old equipment, to tackle farmwork creatively and make the most of situations. Accept, adapt, adopt. That's how he and many Japanese Americans survived. I believe that's why he and I worked well together when I came back from college and started us at the bottom of the learning curve for organic farming. I wanted to grow crops without herbicides, fungicides, or pesticides. So, since I had inherited my father's passion for hard work and his love of heirloom fruits, we became partners. Dad allowed me to farm with alternative, unproven methods, and we made mistakes together, learned as a team how to farm differently. Dad taught me the power of recognizing problems, analyzing them, and identifying new ways to go about things.

We have finally begun to make headway in the fields and the market. Recently, we'd begun to be rewarded for our efforts by the increasing number of consumers of organic fruit who demand authentic flavors. The delicious tastes and aromas that Dad and I seek in our fruit cannot be mass-produced or manufactured. They come only from nature—and authentic work. They stem from a joint effort between farmers and our living materials—often more artful effort than applied science. In spite of our progress, however, we'd come to a point where the only way I knew how to meet our own and our customers' expectations was to work harder. But if we kept going as we were, we would soon reach a breaking point. Farming necessarily takes part in the cycles of life and death, but we organic farmers want to concentrate more on the former than the latter, on growing life-giving food with life-enhancing methods. We want to bring life to fruition, to be part of the creation and preservation of good things. We want to take joy in our work, not kill ourselves with it.

Yet organic farming continually challenges us: We have to weed by hand, and readjust our equipment to accommodate different scales of operation and procedures than those on automated industrial farms. We monitor our crops constantly in order to get rid of worms and insects before they proliferate and take over. Plant diseases—molds, fungi, viruses—demand that we experiment with simple but unreliable treatments. All our methods take vast amounts of time—plus we have to anticipate the weather, react quickly to changes in temperature and wet and dry conditions, and always, always respond to nature, when she is predictable and when she is not. The rewards, though, are wonderful: we have saved from extinction distinctive heirloom peaches and nectarines whose nectar explodes on the palate, as well as grapes that make sweet, plump raisins.

Dad is a gentle, quiet father. I believe that he was happy when I took over the farm two decades ago, but he rarely expresses it. I sense that it pains him to see me work so hard. He knows too well the toll of all this physical exertion. He rarely complains; I only hear from Mom about his long, restless hours of back pain as his body ages.

I walk up and stand next to Dad by the tractor, and we lean together toward its thundering engine to listen. Then I look at his face. He is having a stroke: the right side of his face droops, his eyelid almost sealed shut, his eyes glazed. He looks lost and he doesn't recognize me.

As he begins to limp around the tractor, I hold on to him, trying to keep him from stumbling, falling. I don't know what to do, but think I should first shut off the engine and then get him inside the house. I feel responsible. In my drive to grow the perfect peach and the sweetest raisins, have I contributed to this sudden illness of my father? Could he die because of me?

I manage to turn off the engine, and as the tractor rumbles to a stop, I try to maneuver Dad inside. But he fights me, insisting on returning to his tractor. Still in shock, I give in to his will, feeling such guilt. Dad reaches for the tractor-seat cushion. At the end of the work day, we traditionally flip up the pad so that the morning dew will not collect on it and bother the next driver. With a trembling left hand, he flips it, then allows me to guide him away, his right arm—his dominant hand—dangling as if lifeless. Together, we limp toward the farmhouse.

A few days following Dad's stroke, I discover tracks into the farmyard from what I believe may have been his last tractor drive. The soft dirt captures his weaving and swerving as he frantically returned from the vineyards.

Dad had been working the vines with our tractor, dragging a tandem disc that plows weeds. Our yellow tandem has sixteen circular blades divided into four gangs. The two halves of this equipment mirror each other, which is why it is called a "tandem." The gangs are adjustable so we can extend them wide to cut weeds that are closer to the vines, or keep them centered down the middle of the rows. At this time of year we set the disc out wide so that it can reach into the vine berm to plow under small weeds before they grow larger and become even bigger problems in a few months.

Disoriented from the stroke, Dad parked the tandem and tractor behind the shed at an odd angle. Big chunks of a couple of old grapevines that had been torn off are lodged in the right front gang.

The tire tracks lead from the shed down two short avenues. The twisting trail is not hard to follow but painful for me to see. Dad struggled so hard to steer straight as his brain was assaulted by the stroke.

I trace the tracks back to rows 25 and 26 in our oldest vineyard, a nine-acre block that we called the Eleven-Foot Vines. The rows there are spaced eleven feet apart, whereas in most modern vineyards the spacing is wider, typically twelve feet, in order to accommodate larger equipment. Horses and mules may have worked well in eleven-foot rows, but not tractors. Because all our other vines are spaced at twelve feet, we always have to adjust equipment like the tandem to fit these narrower rows and avoid the risk of taking out a vine.

Half of these vines are close to one hundred years old. When originally planted, there had been forty vines in each of the sixty-five rows; but these rows contained seventy-five vines each. Dad and his brother, my uncle Alan, had extended the rows in 1953, a few years after Dad had bought the farm. In fact, they were planting these new vines when my grandfather, Dad's and Uncle Alan's own father, had a stroke and died on another part of the farm.

Halfway down row 25, three vines have been ripped out of the ground along with their metal stakes. The trellis wires are snapped, the stakes bent and tossed to the side. Two of the vines lie on their sides, most of their fruit-bearing canes shattered, some of their branches still lashed to the wire. Other canes dangle lifelessly from dead vines, their early pale green shoots already dried brown and dead.

Scattered across the area are parts of vine trunks. When the disc blade crashed into the first vines, it smashed and splintered these trunks, scattering their dark black-and-gray wood; it ripped vine roots out from the soil, tearing them apart. Portions of the bodies of a third and fourth vine lie in the dirt, the rest of their gnarled trunks lodged in the tandem blades back at the shed.

The stroke hit Dad at this spot. It must have caused him to black out momentarily or at least lose control. The tractor veered to the right, hooked the first vine, then plowed into the others.

I can't tell if Dad stopped—the tracks don't look like it. Instead, it appears that as soon as the stroke hit him, Dad realized something major was wrong. He didn't try to untangle the blades from the wire or rescue a vine that had only just been pushed over. He didn't stop to assess the damage or clean up the accident. He tried to steer the tractor out of the snarl of metal and plants, the dirt and dust, and get home.

He must have been desperate. The tracks weave down the row, and I see where the trailing tandem disc bounced off other vines, hooking the bark of some, careening off others. I believe he sensed an obligation—to get the tractor back safely and then get some help.

At the end of the row, he yanked the tractor to the right and negotiated a wide turn down an avenue. The tires rubbed against a cement irrigation valve leaving black scuff marks. Behind him, the tandem banged against the wooden end post, slicing a chunk out of the side.

Gradually the steering became much more difficult as he drove toward the final turn, which would let him head directly to the shed. As he whipped through that last corner, the dirt shot up from the tires, the tractor sliding through the soft earth. He almost lost control. So he overcorrected after that bend, catapulting the tractor in the opposite direction. But he managed to find a middle ground and keep heading home.

As the tractor approached the shed, Dad must have lurched as he fought wildly to stay in control, because the wheels swerved. His hands locked around the steering wheel, wrestling for power, engaged in a struggle for direction. It had to have been terrifying and painful. But he willed himself to complete that journey.

His sole goal had been to go home. He had managed to get back. And that's when later I found him wandering around the tractor, trying to remember how to shut it off. The blood clot had begun to kill part of his brain.

Dad has always carried a determination, a drive to work. It is work and belief in the value of perseverance that has always defined him. These gave him the strength to make it home. Seeing this physical evidence of his enormous inner drive, I'm humbled. And I'm worried about whether he can recover from this attack on his brain, on his essential self. And I worry for us both and for the farm, about challenges we will now have to face.

In pursuing Dad's tracks, I read a silent story. I follow his footsteps even further, trying to discover who he was and who he is. Searching for my father, I question my own life and the kind of footprints that I leave behind, my own tracks forward and backward. I try to retain the imprints of his wisdom, gleaning it from his words as well as his work, from his example and from his presence. In searching for my father, I find the one I hope to become. The one I want to become. And I find something of the legacies we've harvested from the land, those that she has freely, beneficently bestowed on us and those for which we've had to die a little every day.

Chapter Two

THE PRICE OF PERFECTION

IT'S MORE THAN one hundred years since my grandfather Masumoto arrived in America, a young man from Japan with dreams. But near the end of the last century, during a time filled with hope and reflection, I turned forty-three and was still searching for my calling, a passion that drove me. I hoped yet to find it on the farm, working the land. But I needed to come to terms with the human costs of farming, as well as the financial ones, the costs we inherit from our past, and the price it extracts from us in the present.

I farm stories. My main story is about trying to grow the perfect peach.

I want peaches that are even better than the ones from my childhood, when I'd bite into the flesh and the juice would gush out and drip onto my white T-shirts. I was fat as a kid and the juice dribbled onto my rotund tummy and slid down its curved edge before tumbling to the earth, leaving behind stains that could never be washed out. My badge of honor, a rite of passage.

Baachan, my grandmother, showed me how to eat the perfect peach. For as long as I can remember, she had false teeth. Crunchy peaches didn't work with her; she enjoyed the soft, gushy ones. When she found a perfect one, she'd take out her teeth, suck the meat out of the peach, gum it to death, and churn it into a puree in her mouth. The peach sloshing in her mouth made a perfect sound. Her face contorted without her teeth. If she saw me watching her, she'd look up and grin a goofy, toothless smile.

Dad, too, had moments of perfection—peach joy. He would eat peaches in slow motion, as if in a play that required that he pause purposefully between acts. Methodically, he would take a small knife and slice a peach in half, guiding the blade from the stem end, along the suture, all around the body and back to the stem. With a simple twist of his knife, the fruit split in half, the pit popping free (hence the term *freestone* for our peaches, as opposed to *cling* peaches, whose flesh adheres to their pits). In the sunlight, the juice glistened. Dad would hold one of the halves up to his mouth and tilt it, as if he were taking a drink from a chalice. Then he would take a slow, healthy bite, teeth slicing through the fibers and flesh. Perhaps it was a Masumoto tradition, but Dad, too, ate with his mouth open, making a chomping sound as the meat sloshed in his mouth. He only needed a few chews before swallowing a ripe peach, and a soft, contented sigh always followed. For years, I've tried to mimic Dad's ritual, punctuating the end of a perfect peach with a sigh. I've gotten close but never quite right.

Dad and I shared one perfect peach during a desperate time in our lives. I had returned home to the farm in the 1980s to work side by side with Dad and soon married Marcy, a farmer's daughter whose family came to California from Wisconsin. A few years later, our first child was born. The farm struggled to make a profit. Prices were bad and no matter how much we produced, it wasn't enough.

I had begun a campaign to save the heirloom Sun Crest peach, a fat and juicy gem with a stunning, honeyed flavor. They were fuzzy, like all old varieties of peaches, but, unfortunately, they lacked the desirable skin color for produce brokers at the time, who wanted red, red, and more red. Modern peaches were bred to be like glossy, uniform lipsticks, whereas the Sun Crest was elegantly, subtly streaked with shadows of red and blush, like a spring dawn. When ripe, it has a gentle amber glow. Sun Crests lack shelf life:

they don't stay hard and firm in a grocery for years. Okay, actually, produce brokers wanted fruit to stay pristine for merely weeks, but "the harder the better" was their mantra. And "harder" is not "better" for flavorful peaches.

All of the older varieties of peaches had become homeless in the modern marketplace. So we took losses, sold below our costs, accepted "adjustments" (always downward) on the pricing of our fruits, accommodations with the brokers because our fruits were unpopular in the wholesale marketplace. The Sun Crest was blacklisted because it looked unripe next to the modern red hybrids and bruised easily. Every box was reduced by a dollar or two because of the name. I felt as if it were our name on each box, too, becoming blemished, compromised.

These economics threatened the survival of our cherished Sun Crest block of three hundred trees. Dad and I initially had responded like most farmers do: we worked harder and faster, cut production costs, strived for efficiency, stripped down to only the essentials, lean and mean. It didn't help us. Prices remained low.

Then I stumbled upon two neighborhood markets in Berkeley, both owned and operated by Japanese Americans. Like Dad's generation, who often turned to others in their ethnic community, I approached Glenn at Berkeley Bowl and Bill at Monterey Market. They both knew about Sun Crest's virtues, nodded their heads when I asked if they could sell them, and said, "Sure, send me some."

But they couldn't handle the volume from 300 trees (about fifty tons of peaches), so Dad and I chose to pick only 20 trees. Our family carefully packed the Sun Crests ourselves and drove them the hundred miles from the country to the city. We made more income from those 20 carefully harvested trees than from the other 280. Grateful, I wanted to ship my best again at the next harvest and worried how to ensure the repeat business—and the survival of our trees, our farm, our heritage.

"How ripe?" Dad asked, voicing the key question we needed to resolve in order for our customers to get Sun Crests at their peak flavor, and for them to want more.

We struggled to figure out when to pick and package our heirlooms. Because the industry wanted hard fruit and an extended shelf life, other farmers were picking greener and greener fruit. Peaches can and will continue to improve if harvested when mature, but a green fruit will never get better. Our peaches traditionally were sold maturer and riper. Now that we would be getting a good price, however, we had the urge to pick a lot, more than the year before, in order to make money while we could. But our pursuit of the perfect peach helped us to hold back from the common business impulse to make short-term returns.

We held back, partly because a perfect peach requires people who appreciate it, and to reach those people we needed a long-term relationship with Glenn and Bill. The quality of our peaches had to match what Glenn's and Bill's markets wanted: firm enough to be shipped, ripe enough to be enjoyed, mature to the point they kept ripening even after having been picked. So we picked and pondered, *What is right? What's the right maturity? The right quantity? The right relationship? What's the right peach that will convert Glenn's and Bill's customers to wanting more heirloom peaches? What's the right way to save our farm?* Heady questions for two generations of farmers standing in the orchard on ladders.

When we had picked the first bucket, we climbed down from the ladders and studied the fruit. I felt lost: my confidence had been destroyed by bad prices; my lack of experience weighed heavily on me. The taste of failure in my mouth threatened to become stronger than the flavor of the peaches we grew.

Dad picked up one golden peach and wiped it on his shirt. In what would become a new ritual for our first pick of the day, he leaned over and took a bite. Juice dripped, flesh oozed from his mouth. He grinned like a happy child and offered me a bite.

We didn't exchange many words. "They're ready," he said. "Just right."

With the first perfect peach of that season, I rediscovered my passion. I renewed my calling to save the living legacy of great heirlooms and to communicate their histories through flavors and traditions from one generation to the next. Every season finds me continuing to search for perfection. On the surface, it's the feel of the peach. The first smell. The initial bite as flavor explodes in my mouth. The sound and swallow. The second wave of flavor as the aftertaste settles on taste buds. But the peach itself and all its wonderful, unique attributes are only the surface. Each peach represents the fruition of many right actions, each is a story in itself.

In between harvests, I search for the perfect methods to cultivate and care for all the lives that contribute to this ultimate experience of the perfect peach—the living soil, my family, friends, and the workers who help us harvest, our distributors, the chefs and other customers whose ministrations make eating our peaches a communal act.

I also search for perfection in stories, in the full taste of a present moment, in the memories shared with family or friends. When I share these stories, harvested, like peaches, with people who enjoy them, they become timeless, priceless.

Along with this renewed search for perfection came new demands that Dad and I imposed on ourselves. After all, we were still part of a food world in which many farms had become factories, their productivity measured by volume. Many farmers are forced to act more like businesspeople than artisans, their value and the value of their work too often measured by dollars and margins, not beauty, or taste, or the epiphany that emerges from authentic flavor and scent. For almost a decade, Dad and I were not rewarded for our hard, physical work, and our idealistic vision of converting the market to the church of organic heirlooms often seemed impossible. Such brutal, constant labor as ours is not really sustainable, and every year for a decade, I felt something within me die. Survival was our ultimate goal, even beyond our commitment to the environment and social justice. Staying in business was crucial, "Wait till next year" our mantra. I feared that our good causes, like too many, would become a story of failure.

At harvesttimes, I couldn't ignore rising expenses and lousy prices. My stomach tightened; a nausea pushed up into my throat. We were farming the right way, but our noble intentions were leading us into impoverishment. We were rich in values, bankrupt in dollars.

I didn't know what the next step would be. The stories of the past didn't seem to take hold and bear fruit in that homogenized environment of factory foods and plastic fruit. At times, I doubted that I was chasing the right stories. The things we valued here on the farm—hard work, right effort, simple honesty—didn't seem to be worth much then and didn't help sell peaches or raisins. They gave us little comfort when economic realities clashed with our ideals, as we strove to be environmentally responsible. It was about the economy, stupid me. But these values and stories of peaches and of artisanal efforts did ultimately spread and help to save us years later.

When it had been only me and my parents on the farm, I had felt braver about staying the organic course. When Marcy and I married, I thought we would double our passion and spirit for farming. We did, but when we had children, things grew complicated. It had been easy to ignore the reality and consequences of risky farming when I didn't have dependents, but now I needed to try manage the risks better. The year our daughter, Nikiko, was born, 1985, was one of our worst years. Marcy went to work in management at a children's hospital while I took care of Nikiko. At least my hours as a father had value, whereas I lost money during each hour I spent in the fields. We ended that year owing more money than we made; it seemed as if I would have to pay in order to go work in my own orchards and vineyards.

Six years later, when Korio, our son, was born, we were still struggling financially. I worried about the legacy I would leave my children and did not want them to have an inheritance of failures. With each disaster on the farm over the next few years, from a hailstorm or rain to the collapse of a peach market or raisin prices, I felt beaten; my voice and aspirations weakened.

I tried not to lose sight of the prize—the perfect peach and all that it means. But every so often we got stuck, emotionally and physically. A rainy spring would fool us; the ground sucks up the moisture but pools in certain areas to create traps for tractors. We know our land, but not every patch of clay and poorly drained pocket. Once, before his stroke, Dad flagged me down as I drove along one of our avenues. He had gotten his tractor stuck in the mud. Elsewhere, this could have been a light moment, the embarrassment of needing a pull followed by a good-natured ribbing. Teasing your father, what a treat!

But typically a farmer asks for help only after he or she has exhausted all options, having worked for hours with a shovel or popping clutches trying to unearth equipment, often only to sink deeper and deeper. Finally, exhausted, we give up. Help.

Dad's face was flushed, his chest heaving, heart racing. So, wordlessly, I gathered a heavy chain, started another tractor, and met him at the accident site. We said little, hooked the chain, signaled to rev our engines, and started to claw and jerk his tractor free. Progress was so slow, inch by inch. Roaring motors, spinning tires, flying mud. The earth finally released her prey.

Dad was humiliated. I could have suggested that he learn how to ask for help earlier, but farming today forces us to be independent, to trust ourselves, to ignore the dependency inherent in our work. We believe in working alone. Dad vowed he'd never get stuck again. Nothing I could have said would repair his pride.

Just as we struggle to work independently, we often suffer the physical pain of our labors in private. In the summers, weeks of heat waves of over one hundred degrees sucked life from us.

The children would hear me shout from pain in the middle of the night, the same short cry and stirring I had heard from my father. In the darkness, muscles cramped and tightened, stressed and fatigued. We had lost too much liquid, could not replenish ourselves no matter how much water we drank. Our bodies betrayed us. When we should have been resting in the short hours before sunrise, we'd have to leap out of bed, trying to stretch or massage a limb. Our bodies would be unresponsive, muscles fighting us, growing tighter and tighter, the pain deepening. We'd accidentally awaken spouses as we lamely attempted to walk it off, forced our muscles to relax, tried to take control of the uncontrollable.

We knew these invisible pains would gradually pass. But we couldn't ignore the real pain we also felt then—the pain that we no longer belonged in the food chain, the fear that we could be obsolete, expendable.

Often, at the end of a workday, as darkness settled over the valley, I would sit on a bench on the farmhouse porch, sweat drying. Marcy, Nikiko, and Korio often delayed eating dinner, wanting to share it with me. But just as often I wouldn't feel like eating.

As the heat drained from my skin and I could feel the day's work being erased, I would feel that I had accomplished too little and knew that I had so much more yet to do. I wouldn't want to think about the worm pest I had discovered or the length of the heat wave that was making the trees cry for water.

The children would slowly open the door to peek out. Nikiko would boldly step up to me and quietly ask, "You okay, Dad?"

I would nod silently, but they could see I was lying, that their father was physically breaking, just as I had watched my dad work too hard and too long.

Ten years later, however, we are still here, survivors, Dad and I. And Nikiko is assuming the new role of the last farmer. In spite of the physical pain she has seen, in spite of the financial uncertainties and insecurities, it seems she has also inherited our love: love of the farm, love of work, love of peaches, and even love of the real price of their perfection.

Chapter Three

SECOND SONS

On occasion while we were growing up, Dad played poker with us kids. Even with a bad hand, he rarely folded, claiming you have to accept the cards you're dealt.

Both of my grandfathers were second sons. That means little today, since rights of primogeniture are obsolete. But in Japan during the 1800s, being second meant that a son had little reason to stay in the old country because he would not inherit any part of the family farm. A second son was eternally in line behind the first, destined to occupy second place, to have the second choice, to accept the second best. Parents didn't expect as much from their second sons, so they also grew up with fewer obligations and less responsibility, which sometimes granted them more freedom than a firstborn had. Perhaps that's how and why my grandfathers were able to escape Japan.

Born and raised in small farm villages, one grandfather was from the Hiroshima area, the other from Kumamoto in southern Japan. Life was hard on their farms at the end of the nineteenth century and, as young men, they journeyed to America. They left nothing behind and brought little with them, although their hopes and dreams were no doubt greater than their material possessions.

Farmers are not generally considered adventurous, but most immigrants had a pioneer spirit. The word *settlers,* ironically, masks a risk-taking drive that even my quiet grandfathers embodied: a gamble to cross a vast ocean and journey to a foreign land. They faced an alien language, new cultures and traditions, a different religion and god, and a shifting world of industry and business. Some arrivals sought the familiar; Japanese from fishing villages often continued to work the Pacific, albeit from the opposite shore. My grandfathers still worked with dirt, although the soils in California were different from those in Japan, and the weather blew in from the west, not the east. The crops were different, as were the tools to farm those crops. American shovels had long handles and were designed for larger men and women, for instance, and Japanese immigrants had to learn new skills in order to work in a different agriculture.

Japanese and Asian immigrants helped the existing agriculture to excel. Japanese did not transform the new land with their own familiar crops, such as rice, as Europeans did with dairies and small-farm practices that they brought with them. Working with grapes intended for raisins, and with peaches and nectarines, the Japanese couldn't utilize the generations of knowledge they'd gleaned from raising their traditional crops. Even their most basic wisdom must have initially felt foreign and wrong. But they persevered. For their own meals, they planted Japanese seeds in private gardens to grow traditional foods: napa, daikon, Japanese cucumbers, and, eventually, short-grain rice.

Because alien land laws prohibited all nonnative-born Asians from owning land, the issei (first-generation) Japanese in America could not establish themselves, settle, and put down roots. A few circumvented the legal system by forming corporations that could own land or by purchasing farms in the names of their American-born children. But my grandfathers, like most, waited until their sons were adults when, together, they could work as a family, save money, and purchase land. Surviving the Great Depression and its economic hardships, they thought, would eventually lead to the reward of owning their own property. Then good times would flourish.

That was their expectation, that is, until December 7, 1941, when Japan as an Axis power bombed Pearl Harbor and the United States entered World War II. Japanese-American families were interned in relocation camps, our possessions confiscated, even though we were not sojourners and had no intention of going to Japan. We had no allegiance to Japan. In spite of years of hard work, my grandparents and parents were still not able to call America home.

Both my grandfathers died before I was born. Jiichan (Grandfather) Sugimoto, my mom's father, died from stomach cancer in 1942. He was ill as the family boarded the trains in Fresno to take them to the relocation camps in the Arizona desert. Because the camps did not have medical facilities to handle his condition, he was to be dropped off at a hospital in California, but he refused to get off the train and be separated from his family. The authorities didn't know how to handle his case and allowed him to continue. A few months later, he was the first person to die at Gila River Relocation Center, and according to my uncles, the officials weren't prepared for a death. No one knew what to do with the body.

One uncle remarked, "I was glad they didn't build a crematorium in camp."

After much discussion, the family was allowed to accompany the body out of camp to be cremated in Phoenix, then return with the ashes. At least Grandfather Sugimoto died with family around him.

Jiichan Masumoto arrived in America in 1899 and was a farmworker his entire life. During his final years he shuffled through fields he could never own, where Dad would find him some piecework jobs like pruning vines.

Like many first-generation immigrants, Jiichan longed for the tastes of his native land, but because of his age and circumstances, the likelihood of ever sampling those flavors again seemed impossible. But Jiichan overcame the distance when he made himself a homemade still and brewed sake. He never drank too much, but he would disappear every once in a while for a few hours to visit one of the small outbuildings near the barn to check his equipment and, necessarily, sample his latest brew.

I can imagine the old farmworker—skin dark from years in the fields, deep lines cut into his forehead, and bony knuckles and finger joints that held a small cup of the clear liquid, freshly made, still warm. His lips puckered and eyes closed, he'd slurp the liquor, hold it in his mouth for a second, then let it slide down his throat before releasing a huge sigh. Perhaps for just a moment, he returned to his native village in Japan or relived parts of his American life differently, ending, of course, back on our farm, sitting in the autumn sun, with his perfect blend from a homemade still, waiting to be sampled, again.

Old Italian neighbors, unshaven, with stubble and graying whiskers, rough complexions, and deep accents, would drive up in old pickups for visits with my dad, engines chugging loudly, rolling to a stop in the barnyard dust. They'd discuss the weather and grapes, share an unsolicited opinion about farm politics, and end with a request to glean some of our Muscat vineyards for their hearty homemade wines. Dad would grin and nod, "Sure, go ahead."

Once I asked Dad, "When Jiichan Masumoto was alive, did he have any Italian friends?"

Dad made a frown. "Can't say for sure. Jiichan didn't speak any English, so I don't know how he could talk with those old Italians." But, Dad said, sometimes, a few of the old Italians excused themselves and headed back to where Jiichan sat.

Perhaps in my grandfather's final years, the Japanese immigrant befriended the old Italian immigrant, inviting him to sit down and join him for a drink out near the back of the barn. The two would have come from opposite places on the globe and spoken few common words, but they shared a lifetime in the fields as they tasted a special brew of what I like to think was "Muscat sake grappa."

Lips smacked and sighs welled from deep within after they gulped their shots of home brew. One immigrant would nod his head and give an occasional grunt as the other rattled off stories, waving his hands and arms, dramatically illustrating his point. Two old farmers sat under the shade of a tree near the end of summer, toasting to past and future harvests.

But our farm had begun in silence. My father acquired our farm in 1950. During a warm spring evening, Dad drove Jiichan and Baachan in his old car from their rented shack on a rented farm to the land he had just bought. Dad took a huge risk in buying a place of his own. Old and tired, Jiichan approved, but Baachan hated the idea and fought with her son.

Six years earlier, Dad had been drafted into the United States Army, along with thousands of other nisei (second-generation Japanese-American) men. "Can you believe that?" Dad once told me. "Lock up our family behind barbed wire in the middle of a desert and then draft me?" Having completed basic training, he was sailing to Europe when Germany surrendered.

Dad's older brother, George Hiroshi Masumoto, had been drafted in 1941, a few months before the bombing of Pearl Harbor. Even during the confusion following December 7, while the authorities were uncertain what to do with someone whom they viewed as a potential enemy, Uncle George served his country. He joined the 442nd, the all-Japanese American military unit, and died in France from honest German bullets that didn't question his loyalty.

Baachan kept two photos of her lost son. One she displayed near our butsudan, a Buddhist altar. He was wearing his army uniform. The other I found stored with her alien registration card, family documents, and a few letters from Japan. She had carefully tied the bundle with yellowed string, wrapped them in the faded white muslin cloth, and hidden them in her dresser drawer. The black-and-white photo was taken at Gila River, during a memorial service for Uncle George and the sons of two other Japanese-American families.

I often stared at the silent, still faces, expressions frozen in that black-and-white image. The Masumoto family stands to the right,

Jiichan holding a folded American flag, Baachan a photograph of her dead soldier son. The aunts and uncles are gathered to their right, looking uncomfortable, cramped next to one another, unsure where to put their hands.

Jiichan Masumoto stands erect, his chin out, body stiff. He does not press the American flag to his chest, but loosely holds it in his old farmworker hands. The body of his dead son lies in Europe while he and the rest of his family are exiled in the Arizona desert.

Baachan Masumoto clutches the gold-framed photograph of her dead son, raising it between her and Jiichan, their other five children on her left. Her hands, darkened from years in the fields, are curled around the edges as she tries to hold it steady.

Jiichan seems confused. The American flag droops in his hands. He is the only old man in the picture.

Dad commented, "Jiichan once said that it wasn't right for a father to bury his son."

I cannot know what my family felt. I was born ten years later in a different time and place. But a silence penetrates such gaps, linking me with the past—the silence for my uncle who fought and died for freedom while his parents and siblings were imprisoned in an America that did not want them. For years, my family carried that silence.

Jiichan and Baachan were among the last to leave Gila River. Forced to depart, because the authorities wanted to end this sordid chapter in American history quickly and quietly, they had no place to go. The family had split up: one son dead, two in the army, another had left camp as soon as he could and migrated to Detroit, one daughter had married, and only a young teenager remained with aging parents. Baachan wept as they left because she believed that her oldest son would have taken care of things, if he were still alive. Jiichan was in his sixties in 1945, broken by relocation and the realization that his life's dreams would never happen. Baachan, though, was much younger, in her forties, still strong but bewildered by their wartime experience.

Their train ride from the Arizona desert back into California was very quiet. Jiichan would have to try to start over as an old man, Baachan carrying the loss of her eldest son like a wound that would not heal. They would again have to accept their fate. They had no choice.

They returned to Selma, California, a small farm town south of Fresno where they had been farmworkers. There, good friends, the Toris, another immigrant family from Kumamoto, Japan, had a small grocery store in which they could stay for a few weeks until the store reopened.

That's where my dad joined them. He had traded his uniform for the comfort of civilian clothes, thinking he could finally relax. "Like taking a nap in the middle of the day if I wanted to," he sighed.

But Baachan interrupted any rest and said, "You have to do something. The family can't stay here much longer. We need work. You have to find a job."

"I had no choice," Dad told me.

He found some farmwork, pruning grapevines, and moved the family into a rented barn on a ranch. Life began to improve. They rented land, moved to another farm with a shack for another year. Dad grew tired of renting, working for someone else. He believed in the simple idea that you won't get ahead unless you own something, and you won't own your destiny unless you own something tangible. My father is a quiet, reserved man, but he believed in himself.

When Dad announced he had bought a farm, Baachan was furious. She scolded him about "the gamble" and how "they can take it away." She worried about losing everything again and starting over. "We have a place to sleep and eat. We have food. Why take a chance?" she cried. "You buy a farm like it was a sack of rice."

On the day they were to move to the new farm, Baachan scolded Dad, "Big mistake. This will make more problems."

Jiichan was happy, however, proud of his son. He climbed into the car for the ride to the new place.

Baachan refused to go. She talked about Uncle George. "If he were here, he'd take care of us. Things would be better."

Dad delivered an ultimatum. "We'll wait until the sun goes

down," he warned. "Then we'll go without you and I'll come back later to see if you changed your mind." He stormed out of the shack and joined Jiichan in the car.

The minutes passed, then an hour. The car grew warm in the evening setting sun. No one spoke. Finally, Baachan came out, some of her personal belongings bundled in a *furoshiki* (wrapping cloth) and the rest in a black suitcase with their family relocation number still stenciled in white: *40551.* Dad opened the back door and helped her load her things. She sat and stared out the window, stroking her face with her rough, callused hands. Together they drove to the farm in silence.

When my older brother, Rodney, was born in 1950, the Masumotos had all settled into life on their own farm. Dad and Mom worked long hours in the fields; Baachan pulled her share of the weight; Jiichan still wanted to work, too, but had slowed down and could perform only a few simple jobs such as watching his grandson and trimming vine cuttings, young grape rootings that needed to be planted.

In the spring of 1953, Jiichan sat in the shade of a yard tree with a series of metal tubs surrounding him. One was loaded with grape cuttings, fragile plants with delicate roots. Jiichan filled another tub with water and rinsed each young vine, then carefully clipped the roots to save a strong taproot. Root-bound vines (roots whose tangential fibers have grown too dense and intertwined to send out new rootlets to seek nourishment in the earth) would not grow well in the new land. Jiichan wanted to stimulate growth but encourage new, deep roots.

In the morning air, he worked with a rhythm: washing, clipping, then soaking each vine. Mom was tying vine canes on the wire trellis in the vineyards so they wouldn't drag on the ground. Dad and my uncle Alan were hand planting each vine in the fields.

Rod was almost four years old and Grandpa's pal. They spoke Japanese and spent hours together. Rod sat with Jiichan, playing with the pile of trimmed roots. Baachan was in the house, probably watching my infant sister. The others worked out in the fields.

Suddenly, Rod bolted into the house, yelling, "*Taoreta! Jiichan taoreta!* Grandpa fell down!" He added, "*Jiichan mizu!* Needs water!" Baachan darted outside, saw Jiichan slumped over and on the ground, and ran out into the fields to fetch her sons.

Rod pushed a chair up against the kitchen sink and pulled himself up. Grabbing a glass, he turned the faucet handle and filled the cup. Then he slowly climbed back down, trying not to spill but rushing as fast as he could, trying to help his grandfather with one of the few things he could offer, a drink of water.

Dad called the family doctor, the same country doctor who had delivered my siblings and would deliver me. But he gave bad news that day: Jiichan had had a stroke. He passed away before the end of the day. Dad said Jiichan died on his own place. According to Mom, after Jiichan's death, Rod stopped speaking Japanese. Today, he doesn't recall ever knowing a foreign language.

Following Jiichan's funeral, Dad finished the planting his father had been working on when he died. Today, those healthy, lush vines are rooted deeply in the ground and produce heavy crops of juicy grapes under a harvest sun. Every year, as I work that vineyard, this grandson remembers its stories.

One summer in the 1960s, my parents told Rod to leave the farm and to go to college. He was a junior in high school; I was four years younger, a chubby kid in the seventh grade. It had been a brutal harvest season, even worse than usual. Every season, it seemed, the prices of either peaches or nectarines collapsed, yet we still picked and packed the worthless fruits, losing money. The prices we received were less than the costs of harvest, sorting, packing, and shipping. We would have been better off letting the produce rot in the fields, but we never did. I don't think Dad wanted to see his crop abandoned.

But that summer, Dad stopped paying attention to the market

reports and updates on the prices of fruit. The harvest was late, delayed by a cool spring, and the normal market patterns were out of sync. Everyone else seemed to have a huge crop, so there was too much fruit for too little demand. No one wanted our peaches.

One evening, Mom and Dad talked a long time in the shed. As the daylight faded, they called Rod over. I was playing outside, taking advantage of the cooler evening temperatures after a day of working in the shed with the family. In low tones, almost whispering, they talked about how bad the prices were; no matter how hard we worked, things wouldn't get better. Mom was going to look for work off the farm. There wasn't a future for Rod on the farm. They told him to work hard at school and go to a good college.

Rod nodded. As the eldest son, always very responsible and bright, he lived with certain obligations: he was the first to learn how to drive a tractor; the first to do heavy work like loading the truck with our day's peach harvest; the first to be in charge of the workday's tally for the different sizes and number of peach boxes we packed and prepared for shipment. Now, he'd be the first to leave the farm.

Rod's brilliant scientific mind took him to Caltech, after which he made a good living with computers, integrated circuits, and high technology. Years later, as a Father's Day gift, Rod presented Dad with a small plastic case, inside of which, mounted on white foam, was a gold-and-black integrated circuit that he had designed and put into production. Dad studied it, although his callused fingers and mildly arthritic hands had trouble steadying the small box and his eyes could not focus clearly on the tiny lines crisscrossing the shiny surface. He listened to his Rod tell him of his achievements, and congratulated him. I, too, was proud of my brother, but the technology was beyond me. I think my brother realized then that our simple life on the family farm is very distant from his own.

Our farms in America are homes to second sons: my grandfathers, my father, and me. After World War II, Dad came home from the army to discover a mess, his siblings scattered across a nation, his father an old man, his mother deeply scarred by internment. He returned to farming and created our first family farm in this country. Although I was not expected to take over the farm and didn't anticipate returning there after college, I have followed my father into our business. When I came home, I, too, felt like an immigrant in our fields, a beginner, as my father must have felt. Dad had the additional challenge of mediating between two worlds, between the government he'd served and the government that had virtually destroyed his family; between the old world of more traditional family practices and the new realities of a growing, national market; and between his dream of independence and his ties to the land and family. Dad never folded, but played the hand he was dealt. Like my grandfathers and father, I, too, am a second son, mediating between two worlds, modern and traditional, chemical and sustainable. I play my hands, but I try to have more than one game going at a time so that if I have to fold one, another story will continue for us all.

Chapter Four

THE LAST ORCHARD

I SOMETIMES HAVE A dream that all the farmers in America are lined up in a single column, the oldest first and the youngest last. I then look behind and see very few behind me. Some others may join, but company here at the end of the row remains sparse. I suddenly get that sick feeling that you have when you think you're standing in the wrong line. I miss the sense of safety in numbers.

Awake, I drive through the countryside past farms and think of their owners; only very old faces come to mind. I go to a local Farm Bureau event and don't meet many new farmers. In our little Japanese-American community of Del Rey, in the sixties and seventies, thirty or forty farmers grew crops and reared families. Now I'm one of the few taking over the farm. One bittersweet benefit of this is that, no matter how old I am, I'll still be considered the "young" farmer.

In 1993, four years before his stroke, as Dad and I planted an orchard, he casually said, "This is the last orchard I plant." I wondered if he were passing on a decision-making role to me, or telling me that I'd have to assume responsibility for shaping these trees. After his stroke, I wondered if he'd had a foreshadowing of it, if he had counted his years and compared them with the youth of the trees.

I worry about our country's aging agrarian population and the loss of farmers. The national average age of farmers is fifty-five years old. According to census data, in 1950, just 30 percent of farmers were older than fifty-five. Later, in the 1990s, that number increased to 60 percent. As farmers have gotten older, young farmers have failed to join their ranks. In the 1950s, the decade I was born in, the farm population was over 25 million, with 5.3 million farms. By the 1990s, farm population plummeted to under 3 million, a little over 2 million farms. Farms have grown in size; farmland was still worked, but its farmers were lost.

At the annual meetings of our raisin cooperative, Sun-Maid, they serve a free lunch, so a thousand farmers turn out for this annual greet and treat. Over the years, however, more and more of the audience has gray hair or no hair, and the PA system has become more and more important for carrying out our business. The average raisin grower in the United States is in his sixties. Maybe even older.

When I went to college, I escaped the valley and the farm, leaving Dad to keep farming until he no longer could. My brother, Rodney, and Shirley, my sister, had no intention of returning home. Tens of thousands of farms across the nation shared our family situation. I'm sure Dad thought at times that he would be the last farmer from our family. And neighboring farms were being bought by larger operations that resembled corporate farms, so he may well have also believed he was the last farmer on this land.

When I returned, I too looked around and felt that I'd be the last farmer. Yet only when Dad mentioned, "This will be my final orchard," did I begin to worry. Did I know enough to take over? When would I be ready to farm by myself? Now that I am well along on that journey of succession, I try to articulate what our line means—as a farmer, son, and father. I try to listen to Dad and try to hear what is not spoken, the inner wisdom and the learned wisdom, the values and perspectives.

Some people inherit material objects, homes, land, savings. During the two decades after returning to the farm in the 1980s, I gradually bought half the farm from my folks. I'll eventually get the other forty acres, but I have inherited two other tangibles from my parents: love and fear. Love of the farm. Love of work. Love of the simple things in our world. Fear of intolerance. Fear of politics. Fear of slipping backward. I'm sure there are more ways to describe my inheritance, but "love" and "fear" capture the emotional legacy I now carry. I think of using the word *hate* instead of *fear,* but that connotes tension and pain; hate was not often part of our household. Our fears make us more inward, less assertive. We love with a quiet passion, less public and more private. In our world, actions speak loudest.

Growing up, our home was filled with a simple worldview but with a complexity that may have stemmed from being Japanese and Buddhist. We didn't have ten commandments to help guide us with farmwork or life's work. Right and wrong never carried the weight of sin. Our actions would not lead eventually to a judgment day.

Instead, my parents carried the baggage of the past into the future. Karma—the basic law of cause and effect—ruled a lot of our actions. Instead of the word *Karma,* however, my parents often used the Japanese term *bachi,* which roughly translates into "what goes around, comes around." I often heard: "Take care of trees and vines, and they'll take care of us." Dad sometimes repeated, "Mistakes in the spring will never go away. You'll follow them all the way into harvest."

"Life has consequences" was their message, which communicated the importance of personal responsibility more than any other force. They gently yet persistently reminded me. "Work carelessly and things will break, then that's *bachi* on you." "Forget your homework and you won't do well on the test, that's *bachi.*"

This philosophy worked quite well with farming, where nature and human nature partner. We never wildly celebrated success; after all, a good harvest was a product of many things working for us during prior seasons. We also never had absolute failures; bad news was a result of multiple forces working against us. We didn't need to assign blame.

In spite of lost income, low income, or no income, after every harvest Dad and I prepared the land, pruning our trees and vines, for the next spring. After one year's harvest in which our peaches were damaged, we didn't even wait for the first frosts but headed out while yellowing leaves still dangled on the limbs.

For most farmers, the autumn chill signals a more leisurely season. When each tree is silhouetted against a gray, overcast autumn sky, shorter days should be accompanied with a slower pace of work. We should take the time to shape each tree properly, individualize each one to help it adapt to its place in nature's climate. Yet that winter we labored with a sense of urgency and cut and sliced with speed. We attacked each tree and vine as if battling through a jungle, rather than acting as its steward. Each motion carried an added meaning: we needed to survive.

Good pruning cuts out old wood in order to leave space for the new and severs branches and canes that drain energy away from the main fruit-bearing arms. While pruning, we envision a tree's or vine's optimal shape and capacity for blooming and fruiting, and we want to leave behind strong wood that will bear the best fruits. To work in winter implies that we can envision a future, our eyes looking toward the next season. Instead, that year, we saw only our own desperation. We whacked and chopped, then moved to the next and the next. We didn't stop, didn't hesitate, didn't reflect. We kept on working to keep working to get done what can never be finished.

We made mistakes. We fought the cold and rains of outdoors, in weather that causes accidents, instead of staying inside. We tried to reposition a branch but bent it too far; it snapped and could not be replaced. We'd have to live with that gap in the tree for an entire year—and empty spaces equal no income. As I reached and grabbed another limb, a protruding stick jabbed me in the eye. I blinked, felt no blood, and continued. Hours later the eye swelled and closed. The next day, I worked with one eye.

Temperatures lingered in the thirties, no sun, cold but not freezing, chilling without the feel of sunlight on your face. As fog rolled in and dew formed on leaves and branches, shaking a tree brought a personal rainstorm. The dampness was continuous, pervasive; it chilled our bones. A cane or branch snapped free and slapped my face, the sting immediate. I fell to my knees in pain.

Working too fast, I sliced my hand, hooking flesh on a jagged branch. The protruding dagger had been lying in wait for the naive young farmer, the wood dark and dead, hidden and invisible. Too pressed for time to get a saw, I then tried to cut a fat branch (more like a limb) with my pruning shears, felt my back strain and something inside snap. Tomorrow's work would be accompanied by more pain.

On those winter days, we worked alone in the fog. Dad would trudge home after a day in the fields, his pace slow. Not a march with a deliberate step; his boots dragged, soaked with moisture, pant legs dark and wet. Shrouded in the damp cold, he would seem lost for a day and return tired, almost disoriented. Beaten. Years stolen from him. I felt as if I were being robbed, too.

In spring we want rain but not too much, because moisture will bring pathogens and disease. Dry springs create a race to disk the ground—break up the packed dirt around the trees—before it grows so hard that a cultivator or plow can't penetrate and water won't reach the roots. With a wet spring, weeds appear overnight and taunt us as they grow higher and higher with warming weather. We would try to keep up and also to plan ahead.

A few months after Dad's stroke, I clear a small block of old trees in order to replant new ones. Before Dad got sick, I had replaced a fairly recently developed but still very good hybrid, Elegant Lady, with an even older heirloom peach called Flavor Crest. So now I'm actually replacing the new with the old. I had kept part of the Elegant Lady block, planted in the 1980s, because this peach performs well, has very nice flavor, and isn't as demanding as the heirlooms. The Flavor Crest peach, however, has a superior taste and it ripens in mid-June, when I have no other variety. And the flavor! I can get passionate about Flavor Crest's beautiful honeyed taste, its round acids that are perfectly balanced by sweet nectars.

I need to burn the Elegant Lady trees, now piled in stacks, to prepare the land. It's raining lightly. Our valley air, trapped between two mountain ranges, often becomes polluted from vehicle emissions and other sources, including agriculture and dairies. But with the passing weather front, showers and clean air migrate into our basin. I'm allowed to burn our old trees because it's raining. A contradiction—I will see which wins, fire or water.

Meanwhile, I remain in between. Not old, not young. Following my father's tracks but creating my own path, too. Isolated by the work, but part of a larger community. Ground down by the labor, but buoyed by the pursuit of perfection and its full moments of indelible satisfaction.

When my father mentioned his "last orchard" many years ago, he was acknowledging that death was inevitable, recognizing his love of his farm and the fear of it ending. When death came visiting with Dad's stroke, it just wasn't his time; and, thankfully, he has kept on loving and working his farm. I did have to take over, but we learned to work together in new ways and reestablished our legacy on the land.

As Dad took care of the trees and vines, and they gave back to him, they have also given back to me. And they will give back to Nikiko. To the extent we could, we have made our own Karma, a good *bachi.* When by myself on the land, I can still find moments of pure pleasure: sunrise reflected in a gold peach streaked with red; the sounds of green things growing; the feel of the sun on the trees' branches and grape leaves, warming them, nourishing them, sending light shooting through them and into the fruit, filling them with sweet juice; and the scent of raisins drying in the autumn air, promising their truth in beauty, and beauty in truth.

Part Two

When Things Break

Chapter Five

CALLING YOUR FATHER A WEED

WHAT'S A WEED? Something growing in the wrong place at the wrong time, or just something no one wants? Ralph Waldo Emerson once declared, "A weed is a plant whose virtues have not yet been discovered."

With his stroke, has Dad become a weed?

"He will die," I heard the doctor say, even though he wasn't that direct. Our family doctor, who had delivered our two children, had actually said, softly yet clearly, "In my opinion, he won't recover."

The doctor avoids saying "vegetable," but we are thinking it. Dad has been unconscious for several days. "He might become a vegetable," Mom finally says. It is her worst fear.

We share an image of keeping Dad alive in a vegetative state: tubes sticking out of arms and cavities, fluids pumped in and out of the system, a ventilator artificially breathing for the body. To a farmer, however, the word *vegetable* carries different connotations—after all, we spend our lives tending and nurturing plants. Fruits and vegetables are the ultimate expression of life for certain plants. Taking care of Dad as a vegetable implies something very different to us than to others. But seeing Dad as a weed is more complicated. A weed's life saps energy from other lives around it.

Dad would die. But the doctor does not say when.

As Dad lies unconscious, he breathes on his own and tosses, sometimes even groans. He keeps raising his left arm and hand to his forehead, then rubbing the skin and pushing his fingers through his hair. Does his head hurt? I start to stroke his head and hair, too. "Is he in pain?" Mom asks. The doctor says no and even crudely demonstrates by pushing his thumb into Dad's throat without getting a reaction.

Where do we take Dad to die?

After several days unconscious, he no longer requires acute care, according to the doctors, and his hospital insurance coverage will end soon. We ask what other families have done and we're given a list of acute care nursing homes to consider and visit, the kind of place he vowed he'd never end up in. If Dad had a final request, it would have been keeping him out of "one of those places." We are faced with a decision.

Can we bring him home to die? As a family, we had not talked about that possibility in detail. Dying with dignity sounds simple, but we're not prepared to deal with the specifics of what he would need. How do we get him home? Which room do we put him in, and what bed? How do we care for him? Get him to the bathroom? Change his catheter? What would happen in a medical emergency?

Death is easy. Dying is the hard part.

Perhaps if we had had more time to consider all this, we would have been more prepared, but just a few days ago, Dad was out sweating in the fields, driving a tractor up and down the vineyard and orchards, helping me with the endless farmwork. On our family farm, we are accustomed to being productive; we grow things that need a lot of attention and we harvest them. We harvest intangibles from our labors, too—and satisfaction, love, pride, beauty. We are prepared to care for things, especially one another. But we did not anticipate that when we brought Dad home it would not be for recovery and therapy—we did not anticipate that Dad wasn't going to heal.

One evening, I sit with Dad and convince Mom and my sister to go rest. This is the first time that Dad and I have been alone since he first had his stroke. He still shakes his head occasionally, then swings his left arm out to bring his hand up to his forehead. He mashes it hard against his forehead, as if he's trying to rub out something in his brain. Or am I just imagining this? His right arm still lies lifeless, never moving.

I grab Dad's left hand and squeeze it, looking for response. I run my fingers over the cracks and bumps in his fingernails. There are a lot of stories behind the deformities in his nails. I imagine a hammer struck one and forever left an indentation. Another finger must have got caught or jammed in a box and smashed; it's been flattened for as long as I've lived. A bent, curled fingernail shows signs of having been mauled by a piece of equipment, a trailer hitch or a tractor PTO (power take-off) that slipped and crushed it. So many incidents that I wish I'd known about, that I wish I'd asked him about. I rub the rough spots on Dad's hands, kneading the scars and bumps he's grown from his history on our farm.

Dad's callused hands and fingers remind me of his mother's scarred, rough old hands, the skin toughened where a shovel handle had rubbed repeatedly, extra padding from where a pruning shear rested, layers of skin piled thick so that they can protect. Calluses, not blisters, from working with the dirt and weeds, the shoveling that never ends. Baachan's hands also told a story of struggle, bittersweet and lonely. She had stayed with us after my grandfather died in 1952, then lived with an uncle, then back with us. Baachan remained quiet, never learning English, ever alone in a foreign country that treated her as an alien. For forty years she worked silently, laboring without benefit of a partner, lifting heavy things and completing repetitious chores by herself. Her calluses came from working alone, from persevering with dignity.

I hold my father's hand, something I've never done before. I had grown up rarely shaking hands with Dad and never hugging. Physical touch was not part of our upbringing. Japanese bowed to each other. Working next to Dad daily, we had no real reason to shake hands. Touching Dad is new. Sitting in the dark, enveloped by silence, I feel his hands, reading them, trying to learn stories I may never hear in words.

Darkness arrives early in February. The daytime feels like spring, but the evening reminds me winter has not yet let go. Now, as the evening slips over the countryside, Dad's room grows dim; we sit in shadows; only a small light above his head keeps the darkness away. Yet except for the occasional beeping from a monitor, it doesn't feel like a hospital—as if Dad and I are in a place somewhere between day and night, a liminal space between light and dark.

Since the stroke, we all have continued to talk with Dad. We don't know for certain if he can hear us, but Mom speaks of everyday things, asking if the blanket covering him is warm enough, if the light is too bright, and should she close the drapes. It occupies her and she fulfills her need to care for him. My sister speaks less, but her training as a nurse compels her to ask formal questions. She asks how Dad is feeling, where it hurts, do his feet feel cold? Sometimes her emotions blurt out: "Dad, are you okay?" He lies in place, unresponsive. Rod has driven up from Southern California; he patiently listens to all of us and the doctors but says little.

Now, alone with Dad, in the growing stillness and quiet of the hospital, I fight the urge to leave and go home. What good am I doing? Little to show for hours of sitting around. But I feel I need to stay and talk. I tell Dad about my day in the fields.

"The weeds. The weeds are everywhere. You know how spring is, Dad. Fools you with warmth, tricks you into optimism. Then come the weeds, even before the first peach blossoms."

I stare at his dark outline in the shadows.

"The farm can use your help."

There's no response.

"How in the hell am I going to take care of all the weeds without you?"

Calling Your Father a Weed

We were both weeding when the stroke hit, both of us on tractors, both of us fighting a fight we can't win. Fools to think so. Fools to keep battling. And they do fool you, the weeds.

They tease you with their gentle yet crisp color of green. They're pale and clean, pushing up through the crusted topsoil that had been packed by winter rains, its surface still damp. Weeds are the first signs of spring, almost welcome after the weeks and months of our gray fog. Sunlight breaks through the overcast skies and sprinkles the earth with warmth, stirring seeds to life.

For about two days, tired of the brown, exposed landscape naked of life, I like the weeds' hue. Lush cover crops grow in between the vine and orchard rows, clovers and vetches and legumes that thrive in the cool, moist weather of winter. These green strips are full of nutrients and habitat for critters, a salad bar for the emerging beneficials, such as lady beetles migrating down into the valley from the foothills or green lacewings awakening from their winter dormancy. As the weeds emerge, however, they carpet the land between the cover crop rows. At first, they complement the color scheme with their subtle tone, painting themselves as gentle companions to the first days of spring. Then they keep growing, keep sprouting and racing to capture sunlight. They sprint to reach up and compete with cover crops, spreading their roots to steal water from the vetches, casting shadows over the low-growing clovers without any apologies, showing their true colors.

Some farmers battle weeds with herbicides and preemergents that supposedly kill seeds before they sprout. Yet a few weeds have outsmarted this technology and are now resistant to chemicals. With or without herbicides, these tricky devils tower above vineyard canopies as if taunting us all with their will to survive.

Dad spent a lifetime battling these forces, first with shovels and mules, then with tractors and herbicides. Since I returned to the farm from college years ago, however, we cut back on chemicals and now no longer use them at all, in keeping with the CERTIFIED

Organic line on our packing labels. Shovels, plows, and disc blades are our new/old weapons of choice as we fight the same enemy. We humor ourselves with the military metaphor: war implies winners and losers, those who are vanquished. But in this battle, how can we ever really win? Weeds are part of the system in which we live. Yet we see them as consuming us; they are always there lurking, haunting, tormenting. We have regularly felt the terror of finding a puncture vine gone to seed, knowing that we'll find the plants year after year after year, their thumbtack-like nutlets literal thorns in our sides, their tough taproots requiring time and more time-consuming work to remove by hand.

My organic farming strategy demands precise timing; our window of opportunity to get to weeds is while they're young and fragile. Control as many of them as possible early, and a simple plow or shovel will suffice later in the year, but if we delay now, in the spring, and allow them to thrive—and in some cases we don't have options or time—they'll get too big to hand-weed, too thick for a single blade, or too dense for a plow to get all the roots and seeds. Early spring for us always means that we wage a war of wills, a race against time, a fight against extinction in a garden of good and evil.

I have regularly called in Dad to help when I'm behind and overwhelmed with unfinished work—with weeds shooting up and swaying in the spring breeze as if to taunt me, with peach blossoms blooming and grape buds swelling with the first feel of warmth that sets nature in motion, as well as her demanding calendar. That's when I beg for help. And answering my plea fits Dad's willingness to help me. He never has turned down one of my requests to work long hours and has often labored late into the evening. I've felt guilty, when, coming in at the end of a tough day, I've shut down the tractor, only to hear in the distance, on the other side of the farm, Dad's tractor patiently churning, up and down the field. He would slow at the end of a pass, then rev the engine to initiate another row. Wishing that he'd stop, I'd turn my head, hoping to hear his tractor motor shift into a high-pitched whine that would signal that he's no longer pulling the disc, but instead heading home at high speed, ending another workday. But I'd frequently trudge inside to wash up, my conscience lingering with the sound of Dad still out in the fields, fighting another row of weeds.

A seventy-five-year-old father should be doing better than lying here in a coma in the hospital. An old farmer should be valued more than as just my hired hand. How can I possibly calculate the full value of his work to me as a farmer and as a father? And how can I calculate the costs of this injury he's suffered—especially since it may cost him his life? Have I worked him too much? Turned him into a weed?

Dad had actually mastered his relationship with weeds, learned to take them in stride, to do what he could. Of course, he favors his shovel the most, the handle smooth and cool to the touch, oiled by his hands over the years, the steel blade's silver edge polished from slicing into the earth over and over for each weed. In organic farming, even after a disking, some weeds escape our implements, especially those that discreetly hug a vine or tree trunk. Even after parking the tractor and disc, Dad would sometimes spend a few minutes shoveling a few more vines before heading in for dinner. It's a quiet, still moment without the roar of a motor, the speed of an engine: just the sound of metal scraping dirt and calming breath. You work by yourself, in solitude, happy, alone.

In Dad's lifetime the farm has progressed from shovel to machine to chemical and now back to hand labor. I still have a lot to learn from Dad's way of shoveling, yet I still grow impatient at the uncontrollable weeds. I just want to fix the problem and move on to the other work we have to do. But weeds are always going to be part of our work.

I don't even know many of the names of the hundreds of weeds populating our farm. I have to figure out which are the worst and I have to call a truce with the rest.

I have to learn how to live with some of these weeds and to learn from them.

Dad drifts off to sleep, no longer restlessly rubbing his head. The hospital monitors beep regularly. He is stable. I can leave now. Outside, the night is cool but warm enough to drive home with car windows open. I can sense the weeds growing in my abandoned fields, my tractors and shovels idle. Should I bring Dad home to die with his weeds? Some members of our family may feel uncomfortable with that decision, and, logistically, his and my mother's own house and its small rooms present problems for home nursing. The shock of his stroke has also made us emotionally shaky, unsure we can manage.

My eighty-year-old farmhouse, however, has larger rooms that could work. It is a quarter mile from my folks' house, off the road, tucked behind a block of forty acres. Traditional farmhouses, including that of my in-laws in Wisconsin, often have a parlor for hosting visitors, staging meals, and, as they did a generation ago, displaying bodies and coffins for families, neighbors, and relatives to visit, view, and pay their last respects.

My last act for my father could be to bring him home one final time.

When I get home and slip inside, everyone is already asleep. I wake up Marcy and lie next to her with my clothes still on. In the darkness we talk. There's been no change in Dad and it's time for a decision. What does she think? And how would the kids feel, their grandfather dying in their house? I cry. Marcy hugs me and whispers it's the right thing to do.

The next morning, before they leave for school, I take aside Nikiko and Korio one at a time. How do you phrase the question other than the obvious? "I'd like to bring Dad, Jiichan, home for his final days. He'll die here."

Korio is just five years old and struggles with the concept. He sees his father blinking back tears and knows how important this is but can't comprehend it all.

"Okay, Dad," is all he says.

But eleven-year-old Nikiko had heard Marcy and me talking late in the night and earlier that morning about bringing Dad home, so she first asks, "Is Jiichan better?"

I shake my head and ask her my question.

She blinks back tears and says, "That's what Jiichan would want." We hug.

Throughout the day while weeding the vineyard, I prepare myself to talk with my mom, my sister, and the doctors and work out details of the transport and release. We'll need a hospital bed and other equipment to make Dad as comfortable as possible. After work that evening, I'll drive to the hospital and talk to the whole family.

But just as I step in from the fields and the plowing, I get a call from the hospital. "You won't believe this," Marcy says. "Dad is waking up."

Chapter Six

LIVING WITH INSULTS

WHEN DAD WAS in a coma at the hospital, I thought about his passing as tragic, moving. And I thought of how we all die in simple ways, slowly and gradually ebbing away.

I once asked Dad, "What sense is the most important to you?" He answered, "The one so I could keep working."

In the first few days after Dad wakes up from his stroke, he beams at the sight of family. We huddle around his hospital bed, hugging and smiling. He even teases five-year-old Korio by gently pulling on his ear, repeating a playful exchange between grandfather and grandson. I clutch his left hand. We both squeeze. Happy to feel.

His right side is damaged. He cannot lift that arm. His right leg and foot lie limp. He explores his body with his left hand, rubbing his legs, searching for something. When he reaches over and lifts his right arm, the dead weight startles him.

He's trying to assess what's working and what's not. Dad is still alive but something has been stolen from him: none of us knows what he's lost. I worry about his ability to function on the farm—and what part of him has died and what part of him lives. He had built his life on a physical relationship with the world. Would his body now deny him that life?

When they wheel his bed to a lab, Dad sees himself in the mirror and stares. The CAT scan confirms that the blood clot had damaged the Broca's area of his brain, where speech and communication originate. He may never speak again. I rationalize: farmers don't need to talk. Our peaches and grapes do not require conversations, they just demand our presence.

A medical specialist runs a swallow test, to determine if Dad has control of his throat muscles and can eat and drink normally. Otherwise, we will have to feed him forever through a tube inserted in his stomach. We prepare for that reality—and the tragic irony of a farmer never again tasting his produce.

I had never thought of swallowing as a skill, a technique that our muscles have to learn and remember to perform. If Dad has some sensitivity in his throat—if he can feel the liquid—through therapy he can relearn how to swallow. I hope that the years of tactile experience on the farm will help Dad, since he understands the power of the sense of touch. Dad passes the test—with practice, he can have family meals again with us.

Tests and more tests. What are they measuring? What indicators are they looking for? Dad and I both distrust the science of assessment and rarely do soil analyses or leaf and petiole sampling to determine the nutrient deficiencies of our soil and plants. Over decades, we have identified the weak sections of our farm by observing which trees or vines were struggling. We didn't need a test to verify what we already knew. If I had been a better science student, perhaps I'd appreciate agricultural research and evaluations more. Instead, I have been trained, like many farmers, in the human nature sciences, the relationship between emotions and working with nature.

For example, I know that the worst and the best times to make critical plans for the future is in the middle of intense farmwork—with hundred-degree temperatures, sweat sticking to my back, and fluctuating market prices affecting the daily picking of fruit. That's when negative emotions are going to influence my thinking. Most organic farmers don't do what we do for the money. Nor do we work according to well-conceived business plans that take into account the whims of nature—such a plan is impossible. Something else keeps us toiling despite the challenges—our emotional connections to the living things we grow, to the land, even to the people who eat what we produce.

Right or wrong, in the heat of harvest, we do make choices. Emotions belong in our decision making. The dominant measuring stick for most corporate farmers' decisions is profits, but Dad had learned long ago to distrust the significance of profits. He could do everything right in a year, his hard work complemented by perfect growing conditions, and prices could still be bad and profits ephemeral. Good work, important work, necessary work is not always measurable by profits.

As a farmer and eternal optimist, "next year" had been Dad's rallying cry when the weather or harvest was bad. Now, it is also Dad's silent answer to the medical tests. Still hospitalized, his stay extended when he came out of his coma, Dad undergoes daily evaluations, assessing what he has become, although determining who he is will take months. "Six months to see what comes back," the doctors explain. "Things can improve with therapy and hard work."

Hard work will not be a problem. That's why he had the stroke, working long hours, rarely resting, pushing to get one more field plowed and leveled. Along with his recovery support team of health professionals, I make my own evaluations of whether he should now rest or start rehabilitation. But because I still feel guilty about my role in his illness, I worry that I will make Dad part of a new crusade of mine. Having saved heirloom peaches, can I now perform heroic acts to save my father—and myself?

The true test of Dad's recovery will be whether he regains the use of his right side, even minimally. Should his right hand never come back fully, however, I can teach him how to work with his left and compensate for the diminished capacity of the right, because I am left-handed. He is right-handed, like the majority of the world. Perhaps we can create a new partnership.

Mom and Dad gradually develop a symmetry—she can't hear, he can't speak. Mom had begun to lose her hearing a decade earlier and had given up on hearing aids. "They only boosted the noise," she claimed. So now I will have a father who can't speak but can listen, and a mother who can't hear but can talk. Dad has always been quiet, Mom the talkative one, often thinking out loud. Their new post-stroke relationship may not miss a beat.

Alone again with Dad one evening, I massage his right hand, trying to bring life back to the muscles and joints. With much pain and effort, he can now raise that arm slightly. The doctors keep asking if he can wiggle the fingers or toes on his right arm and foot, but he fails each time. I keep thinking there must be a better method of testing, but it occurs to me that at this early stage of his recovery, a lot may be regenerating underground. We were all seeking visible signs of improvement, but unseen improvement could be taking place within his body and brain, much like plant roots growing and preparing to nourish the rest of the plant. I want to believe that nerve cells are multiplying and rerouting themselves, trying to establish new connections in parts of his brain, invisible to the eye, hidden from view, much as a plant takes in nutrients, preparing for a growth surge at the right time.

In his hospital room one evening, without the doctors and nurses and the rest of the family, Dad finally feels relaxed. So I ask him, "Dad, move your fingers."

He looks up at me and I sense he understands what I'm asking. He nods and tenses, straining to make connections, willing his right hand to respond.

Nothing.

I urge him to try again, rubbing his skin harder, feeling his bony knuckles and joints under my fingers. I stop. He tries again. His hand shakes. I can see his muscles straining. But his fingers don't move. I press harder. His calluses feel like lumps of flesh pushing back. I suddenly stop and command Dad; my voice startles even me. "Move your fingers."

He contorts his face, his body tightens. We press forward. Coaching, responding. Pleading, trying. Demanding, answering.

It begins with his little finger, moving slightly. A quiver. A jerk. An uneven twitch. But movement. Visible.

He then works harder, a controlled motion that spreads to his other fingers one by one. Stop. Pause. Breathe. Retest to confirm. Subtle and minor, but still movement. Finger by finger, from the little one to ring, middle, index, and even the thumb.

Exhausted, we stop. He needs rest and closes his eyes; a gentle grin appears on his face. We see improvement. Dad can now dream of work: we have hope.

Our farming will never include many tests. Experiments and observations are daily tasks, but tests with clear results are rare. Tests imply that there are specific, narrow questions that can isolate a problem and thus help us to discern solutions. But so many problems have multiple factors at their roots, complex causes, uncontrollable influences. They are "overdetermined." Nature works too slowly for most people who want answers to tests and questions immediately. Farmers have to work within nature's time frames, however. They accept the consequences of weather and other natural influences, but they try to make up for setbacks and problems by simply working harder. They do everything they can to avoid failing. Dad's stroke has shown me that working harder is not always the solution, but it was the right response for my parents when they ran the farm.

Allowing Dad to fail will be part of his recovery. After six weeks, he is making great strides physically. He still cannot talk but seems to understand more. I hope it will be enough to work the farm. I bring a toy puzzle—a physical test that both he and I can understand—to his room, colored blocks with fragmented images on their interlocking sides. When turned in the proper sequence, they match up to create a caterpillar.

I dump out the puzzle blocks on top of his bedside meal table, and immediately he starts to build his caterpillar. He finds the first two correct pieces quickly. I smile. Then his eyes squint; he's having trouble. The pieces aren't fitting together. He tries one, it's close but not quite. He tries to force it together, knowing it's not right, hoping it will somehow slip into place.

Another one correct. More wrong. He starts to sweat; his left hand begins to shake. His eyes dart from one block to another, trying visually to piece together the caterpillar shape, but when he tries to connect the pieces, the joints don't cooperate and he's forced to try again and again.

Both of us are breathing hard. We sigh and groan with each effort and cheer with each success. I tense, muscles contracting as I follow his intentions. It would be easy to reach out, point, coach, direct his hand to the correct piece. Dad sounds as if he's growling. I'm whispering to myself, biting my lip, fighting the urge to give him help.

By the last two pieces, Dad's not thinking but just striving to finish the task, drawing on the determination that has always been part of his nature. The final piece is snug, the last joint to fall into place, the least worn, a tight fit. Sweat drips from Dad's forehead, down his temples, and off his chin as he joins them together. He blinks, limbs shaking, short of breath, but he succeeds and collapses back into bed. I cheer and pat him, and we share a sense of accomplishment. I had let him fail at the smaller steps so that he could succeed overall.

He closes his eyes and rests. I, too, relax since I now have evidence that Dad seems able to reason well enough to put things together. Another sign of recovery.

I relax for only a moment before I realize that he can put together a puzzle our children did when they were three or four years old. Suddenly, the thought depresses me. *The work of a child, is that the best Dad can hope for? The best we can expect?*

I'm feeling sorry—for Dad and myself. The optimism necessary to farm vanishes. I selfishly believe our operation will have to lower our standards without Dad's help—I can't expect much assistance from him. My thoughts of a perfect farm crumble.

The puzzle goes back into the bag. I hate tests.

Dad appears tired, winded by the last few minutes of work.

I start to vent my frustrations, to rant out loud, a soliloquy about our new limitations and realities as a consequence of his stroke. I try to comprehend what we're up against. We can hope, we can bargain, but how long can I deny the truth: I will farm alone.

Dad stirs, watches me, and listens. Then he grabs my hand and shakes it wildly. The rapid whipping and speed shocks and even scares me. He shakes it again, as if to wake me up. I nod. Dad is there and he does understand. And he's determined to come back home.

A stroke insults the body, the mind, the survivor, the family. Other illnesses and conditions can sometimes be repaired. The heart can often be fixed with modern technology and medicine. Even devastating, once-terminal cancers have an array of treatment programs and options. But a stroke is lonely and isolating, recovery slow and uncertain. Little can be done once the stroke has done its damage—recovery has no magic pill or quick treatment to fix the brain. Rarely do you get back what you lost; rarely are you ever as good as you once were.

I'm angry now at what has happened to my father, at this insult to him and to our lives and livelihood. I know he must feel frustrated, cheated out of his normal life, out of normal conversation because he was working too hard. Yet his therapy will demand even more hard work. The question now is how he and all of us around him will respond. How do we live with this insult?

After another week, his seventh, Dad continues to become more alert, more himself. He responds to physical therapy, even taking a few steps. He will walk.

He recognizes everyone, but I wonder if his "farm memory" was insulted by the stroke. In spite of my dislike of tests, I decide to bring into his hospital room some small farm tools—a crescent wrench, old pliers, a screwdriver; even a small pruning shear we use for grapevines—to see if he recognizes them and remembers how to use them. Immediately, he smiles, grabs the screwdriver, and wraps his left hand around the handle. He holds up the pruning shears and manages to grip one handle loosely with his right hand. He holds it up and opens and closes the blade, as if warming up to do some pruning. I'm hopeful again, although it's one thing to know what a pruning shear does, but another to remember how to prune.

I should not doubt him. He can identify these tools, as if he has reincarnated from his other life, before the stroke. Perhaps now he's retooling himself to a new reality, refitting himself in order to create a new relationship to these old friends.

Dad then picks up the old pliers. And seeing that single, subtle act, I'm relieved and filled with new hope. He holds the pliers in his left hand and immediately and seemingly unconsciously moves his thumb and index finger around the nut and bolt holding it together. We always have had problems with these pliers, the screw is too loose and there's too much play in the tool. So we tighten it by hand before we start a job, just as Dad is doing. His muscles remember; they will help rebuild his brain. The years of hard labor still live in his brain, and they will prove essential for his recovery. A turn of the screw with ghosts—good ghosts of memory, helping Dad come back home.

During the next few weeks of therapy, Dad lives at a rehabilitation center. He makes extraordinary progress, and the family begins to talk of his return to the farm. We all work well with the professional therapists, who seem to enjoy working with Dad. At their weekly staff meetings with us, they share encouraging stories. At one point I bring in a photograph of Dad in the fields so that they have an image of the healthy, accomplished farmer who is also a husband, father, and grandfather. This is the man I hope to get back, I hope we all get back.

Chapter Seven

RESILIENCE

"SHIKATA GA NAI" is Japanese for "it can't be helped" or "there is no choice."

As a child, I would ask my parents about the relocation and uprooting of Japanese Americans during World War II. I wondered how they coped with being imprisoned and why they and others hadn't done something.

Mom and Dad would pause, and silence would fill the space between us. Finally, they would look away and whisper: *"Shikata ga nai."*

Farmers are good at disasters. We've practiced dealing with a lot of them. A history of disasters helps our family cope with Dad's stroke.

When your livelihood depends on nature, you understand how fragile life can be. With any life crisis, the emotions are real, the loss painful, the anger deep, but a natural disaster carries a brutal yet democratic honesty. It spares no one, spreading misery with a wide brush. Each natural disaster creates a vivid memory for a farmer and, perhaps, a lesson. With time and reflection, we distill our memories into healing stories and reinforce them with each retelling. From disasters we learn, we grow, and we change. We learn to accept things that are outside of our control, adapt to the consequences, and prepare for the next time.

The first major disaster in which I played a role was in March of 1972. As a child, I had lived through freak rains and winds during peach harvest and heat waves that caused immature fruit to drop from trees, but in '72 as a senior in high school, I was old enough to know a real disaster. However, escaping the valley occupied my mind, not weather forecasts and a killing cold air mass that had begun moving south into California.

Arrogant and impatient with life on the farm, I was vaguely aware that Dad and Mom were worrying and listening constantly to the radio and weather updates. Outside, the vineyard had grown with the initial warm spring weather, its pale, fresh green shoots reaching upward; some as long as six inches, although most had emerged a delicate two or three inches. Tiny grape bunches were barely visible, pushing out from the shoots.

Like an arctic wolf, the cold air crept into the valley. Although daytime highs were in the sixties, the clear, cloudless evening sky allowed nights to cool rapidly. Spring freezes are tricky, the cold air mass invisible. You might feel a seemingly benign chill in the air by the late afternoon and not recognize it as the breath of a killer. But in the middle of the night, the wolf prowls, then, a few hours before sunrise, pounces—temperatures collapse and the damage is done.

One chilly evening, I had high school track practice, did homework, watched some TV, and went to bed. Dad had been working all day, opening furrows around our fifty acres of vineyards, preparing to coax a little more warmth into the bare, open ground. Green shoots will tolerate thirty degrees for an hour or two, but any lower or longer and the water in the leaves and shoots freezes, the crystals killing them. Dad set the irrigation valves to run water down as many rows as he could. The pump water was warm and could raise temperatures a few degrees, perhaps enough to save a crop.

At dinner we all acted normal—Dad probably didn't want to talk about the pending disaster. Later he went out in the darkness to check the pump, the hundreds of irrigation valves at the end of each vine row, and watch the thermometer. Up most of the night, Dad kept the irrigation water running, and he checked and rechecked the temperature. He wrote numbers on the back of an envelope that he had tossed into his pickup: midnight—36 degrees; 3:00 a.m.—31; 5:00 a.m.—28. Then the numbers stopped. The coldest was right at sunrise, the first light of day becoming a bittersweet moment.

I awakened to frost on the roofs and a fog in the vineyards from the warm pump water condensing in the freezing air. Dad was sitting at the kitchen table, work clothes already dirty and dusty from his long night. He drank his morning coffee in silence. I searched for the right things to say and found nothing. Neither of us said anything.

A freeze takes days to show damage. On that first day, green vine shoots still seemed healthy. After school, I found Dad in the vineyard, looked around, and, trying to fool myself, said, "Looks okay to me." Dad just frowned, then shrugged. Denial provides space for reflection.

But by the third day, the green had turned black. Panning over the vineyard, the dark stain stretched over the low grounds, about a third of our farm. The cold air had pooled there, lurking around the new vine growth and then killing them. In vivid contrast, the green shoots on the higher ground looked like a living carpet.

We lost tens of thousands of dollars of future crop in that one night. The industry as a whole reported a $40 million loss of raisins. The smallest raisin crop in the century was harvested that year. Other fields, too, were damaged, vegetables and strawberries in our valley as well as in Southern California. We were not alone.

I regretted not having paid more attention. I hated the helpless feeling of watching the grapes wither and die, a passive observer of a disaster. I felt guilty about not having kept Dad company on his night vigil—I had been privileged that someone else had had to worry and I hadn't had to think about it. Others may view it as a sign of wealth when you can pay someone else to do the dirty work and distance yourself from the disaster, but I felt that I had lost an opportunity to grow, to learn something about myself and about something greater than myself.

We lived with that freeze for the rest of the year, tending empty vineyards so they'd keep growing for the next year. Of course, prices were outstanding for the few farmers whose crops had not been hurt by the freeze. At almost every community event, farmers talked about that freeze and what it meant, trying to heal their wounds a little, sharing the misery. Even years later, we still talked about that killing frost, the lessons learned, the stories passed on.

I lost some of my naïveté that chilly morning. Humbled, I would carry a memory of loss—not of the grapes or dollars but of innocence. I was still engaged in the disaster whether I liked it or not. I had to accept it. And I also had to accept the fact that I needed to practice paying attention.

When I came back to the farm four years later, in the summer after college, my father welcomed me back by giving me more responsibility than ever. I accepted it but quickly realized that I had a lot to learn if I was going to leave my own mark on the farm.

It didn't take long for more disasters to materialize to teach me further lessons. That fall, and then again two years later, heavy rains came in September, just as we were trying to dry grapes into raisins. Not the "welcome home" omen I was looking for. Nor was it a pleasant start to the farming career I had hoped to create.

To prepare to make raisins, we disk the ground between the rows of vines in August. This clears out all the weeds and leaves behind a fine, powdery, smooth layer of earth. In early September, workers pick the green grape bunches and lay them on the ground atop paper trays, each sheet about three feet long and two feet wide. Typically, the blistering sun and dry heat of central California cure the grapes into raisins in about twenty-five to thirty days. It's a simple, natural process with one major flaw: the potential for rain.

An acre of grapes has about five hundred vines. Each vine produces about forty pounds of grapes. A raisin tray starts with twenty pounds of green grapes that will dry into four pounds of raisins. During raisin harvest, our fifty-acre vineyard will have fifty thousand trays and, if nature cooperates, one hundred tons of raisins.

In 1978 we had a typical crop. We picked the first week in September, and the vine rows became blanketed with green grapes lying in the sun, warming and curing. A week later, the berries had begun to change color, turning darker, almost a translucent violet, and filled the air with a sweet caramel fragrance. To me, it is the scent of optimism.

I watched the weather reports carefully, hoping for the best, but a low-pressure system was dropping from the North Pacific, mixing with the remnants of a tropical depression from the south to create sleepless nights. I kept listening for subtle changes for the good. Predicting weather is tricky; some speak in percentages—a 70 percent chance of rain means seven out of ten times they report it, rain should occur. (Of course, I hoped for the three out of ten times it wouldn't rain.) Weather reports also use the expression "measurable rain," meaning we could get as little as a few hundredths of an inch of rain or as much as a deluge (for our valley in California in September) of a half inch.

Raisins can withstand a sprinkle or light shower, perhaps even a tenth of an inch, depending on how much the grapes have dried. So I slipped into denial. Rains were forecast, but while I anticipated showers, we got thunderstorms that hammered our valley with lightning and more than a half inch of rain, followed by a cool day in the seventies then another storm and another quarter inch.

The grapes had rested in the sun for only a week when the rains came, so they were still more grapes than raisins. The first drops of rain that hit the earth created little puffs of dust. As the drops struck the thousands of paper trays, they created a soft sound—*pat, pat, pat.*

I felt exposed, helpless. I would not be insulated from this storm. This was not someone else's problem. I rushed out into the vineyards to try to protect the grapes, covering them with paper or rolling up the trays like oversized cigarettes. I tore the skin of the delicate berries as I piled them into heaps. Their flesh split, their juice seeping out. I made a mess of a hundred trays before I gave up. Forty-nine thousand nine hundred other trays stood waiting my inept efforts.

I limped home. Dad was inside and watched me return. He

didn't say anything. I told him he was smart not to get wet. He slowly nodded. From his own experiences, he had known my efforts were futile; but he also knew I had to try.

For the next few hours, I paced and roamed in the house, unable to sit still, watching through windows, dashing outside when the sprinkles paused to check the horizon. From the west, the front advanced, the clouds grew darker and darker. There was no hint of blue sky. My hopes for a full harvest were crushed.

When the sprinkles turned into a downpour, I stood by our back door, sickened by the pounding sound. Dad ran out to get the newspaper, where it had been tossed in a puddle. He grumbled about his paper getting wet as he hung the pages over the backs of chairs in order to dry them. I asked Dad, "Shouldn't we try something? To at least do one thing, anything?"

He shot back, "What can you do?"

Dad was right—we had few options. If the raisins had had another week or two of sun and heat, perhaps we could have rolled the trays "heavy," the grapes not fully dry. Later we'd have had to open them again to cure, but at least we could have salvaged a crop. But our raisins were still full of moisture. Moving the entire crop undercover was impossible, too many trays would have to be handled by too many people—the labor costs would have far outweighed the value of our crop.

Had it rained only slightly, we might have had a chance—we could have "slipped" the trays, moving them one or two inches to one side, to reduce the moisture between the paper and dirt where mold grows. We also could have turned over the trays, flipping them to expose the undersides of the bunches to air and sunlight. If all else had failed, we could have hand sorted and removed the raisins that had begun to decay.

But significant rains inflict damage beyond repair: bunches rot, then fester—the stench from this storm would fill the air. Our drenched raisins would sprout putrid, nodular molds that would spore throughout the harvest, destroying all hope. Even the most optimistic farmer gives up in the face of this kind of disaster.

The rain was relentless. For hours I listened to it, soft then intense. Night provided some comfort only because I could no longer see the falling drops, even though I could still hear them. Dad and Mom went to bed, although I doubt they slept. I raised the volume of the TV to drown out the rain's tattoo on the roof, forsaking the local evening news and weather reports I had been religiously following.

By morning the puddles in the yard were huge and there was standing water in the vine rows. The smell of rain still filled the air, although it had finally stopped falling sometime before dawn.

Over coffee Dad and I talked little. I had calculated the economic loss, tens of thousands of dollars, but the numbers meant little. After my third urging, Dad agreed to put on his boots to head outside and assess our losses.

All the trays were soaked. Weakened by the moisture, they would tear if we tried to move them. Each tray was stuck to the wet earth underneath it, and those clumps of dirt fused with paper and rotting grapes would take weeks to dry. In some rows, the paper trays were submerged. Grapes floated in the puddles, their flesh turned white; the mold would quickly follow. Other berries had embedded particles of sand that had splashed up on their surface; they would make gritty raisins if not cleaned. Most of the bunches had absorbed the hours of moisture, so that the grapes had gotten overly fat, their pale flesh stretched. Some had burst and split like open wounds, tissue dripping out; they would fester and rot.

We kneeled down over one tray. Dad picked up a bunch of grapes, shook off the water. The skins had turned a yellowish brown, a rank odor already accompanying the decay. Dad ran his hand over the berries; the skins broke, spitting the meat of the grapes onto his fingers. I asked, "Aren't you mad? Isn't there something we can do?" Dad carefully replaced the bunch, rose, and announced, "I'm not going to crawl around on my knees trying to save this mess. Not for this crap." He turned toward the shed, grabbed his shovel, and left for a walk through his fields.

A few days later, Dad hooked up a disc to our biggest tractor and began going up and down every row in the vineyard, disking in all the raisins, burying them in the dirt, turning them back into the earth. He started early in the morning and took only a few breaks, continuing into the evening and a brilliant setting sun. He worked as if possessed, driven to finish this last job. Mom worried, stepping outside while dinner grew cold on the dining-room table, wondering when he would come in. Occasionally in the distance, we saw the flash and blinking of headlights from the turning tractor.

As night fell, I stood in the yard, listening to the tractor go up and down the rows. I guessed he was near the last vineyard block on the far side of the farm. But something was odd; the normally methodical and slow tractor echoed with a different rhythm. He was driving a little faster, accelerating down a row quicker. I then realized that Dad was angry. But the only thing to do was to work it off. He had no choice.

My disaster learning curve continued. In 1983 we had one of the rainiest springs on record. It rained almost every weekend. Marcy and I were married that spring and, amazingly, the clouds parted for our ceremony. That harvest, however, pathogens demonstrated how well they thrive in humid, moist conditions. Brown rot devastated peaches; mildew rotted grapes.

Other disasters became mere footnotes: Rains pounded the raisins again in 1991. An Easter freeze in 1999 turned green vines brown. A heat wave in 2005 lasted a month, with consecutive 100-degrees days, a few reaching 113 and 115.

When you farm as a family, everyone shares in the disasters. The humbling vulnerability of working with nature exposes us at our weakest moments. When my children were young, they saw me curse at rain clouds and scream at the wind, sympathetic to their father's distress, but not fully understanding what was going on. With each disaster, I tried to gain a sense of history, to put each loss in the context of larger issues. But repeated losses built up emotional scar tissue on top of my experience and learning. Monetary deficits generated burdens I couldn't ignore. Disaster weighed us down, but it also created ties that bound us together.

Dad was correct. Accepting that some things can't be helped compels me to ask better questions. Instead of futile whys, I ask, Given the circumstances, what can I do best? That's when I become aware of the whole, accept that disasters are part of life and adapt so that they contribute to my growth and my family's growth. Trying to do the best I can: that's all I can ask for, that's how I heal from disasters. *Shikata ga nai.* It can't be helped, there is no choice. But I'll always ask, What can I do better?

As a nisei, second-generation Japanese American, Dad had to come back to the farm to take care of his aging parents, the issei, first generation. He didn't have a choice. Ironically, we sansei (third generation) also didn't have a choice. We were expected to go to college, leave the farm, and make ourselves better. A world on the other side of the mountains that ring our valley awaited those willing to leave home and become something. Stay and life will beat you; leave and you had hope.

In the years I decided to stay on the farm, we and other farmers faced a huge surplus of grapes and raisins for the four years that there wasn't a killing frost or harvest rain. As the crops grew to another record size, I marveled at how bad prices got for a harvest no one wanted. Once prices of grapes were announced, dreams of profits quickly faded—another economic disaster. I would pencil out our losses and realize that a year's worth of labor had been wasted, nothing gained. After weeks of crawling on my knees, working with a worthless raisin crop (hearing talk about tons of raisins being used as cheap cattle feed), I concluded that we would have been better off not growing a single berry and letting the vines go wild. Grapes of wrath in a new century.

Nonetheless, I feel I have time. After all, a farming timeline is supposed to be long. A vineyard takes three years to bear a crop, then can last many human lifetimes. Our orchards have produced huge, juicy fruit for more than forty years, an old-growth forest by conventional standards. Besides, someone has to grow our food and learn to work with nature. The disasters give me unforeseen opportunities to grow, too.

In Japanese culture, individuals often carry a tradition of obligation and burden. Typically, outsiders see this as a negative and a sacrifice. Yet my obligation to the land and farm gives me identity. My passion grows with the burden. As a family, we have discovered a security in the ties that bind us—to the land, to one another. We have meaning in our lives and, when I think of another generation on the land, I feel both worried about the burden and alight with happiness at the continuity and potential.

Dad and Mom were pioneers, working in the face of racism, forced to prove themselves to be more American than other Americans. They gambled and bought land, claiming their place on the earth. My wife Marcy's folks left family and Wisconsin to venture to Southern California in the 1950s, hoping to settle down by farming then dairying in the high deserts with herds of goats. They were ahead of their time, before goat cheese became gourmet, before a health food revolution changed palates. They labored in isolation, drawn to goats because of Marcy's allergies to cow's milk, hoping to share their bounty and contribute to a fledgling alternative food community. Lonely pioneers, they were a generation too early.

Compared to these sacrifices, my depression over the intransigent low price of raisins seemed trivial after only four years of nonprofit work. We still have our health. We haven't lost land. Coming back to farm, what had I expected?

On June 15, 1995, my first book, *Epitaph for a Peach,* was published by a major national publisher.

By the end of the second week of June, fleshy peaches were also hanging on branches. In the summer heat, they were swelling and growing fat. I began to believe that my labor could result in a wonderful harvest.

But nature was teasing me. Occupied with dreams of harvest, I did not pay enough attention to weather reports. An Arctic air mass had moved into California and tangled with a tropical jet stream. At worst, I anticipated a rain that the fragile peaches would not like, that might break their delicate skin, making it a breeding ground for rot.

On June 15, clouds shot across the sky with a speed I'd never seen before. They whirled overhead, catapulted by winds that flung them from one horizon to the other. The sky swirled and churned with energy and motion, massive forces flexing above my farm.

From the farmhouse porch, I watched winds whip across the fields. Grape leaves popped inside out like miniature umbrellas flapping in the gale. Trees shook from side to side and bounced up and down, battering fruit against the branches, leaving bruises and scars that would ruin them.

Gradually at first, and then rapidly, with overpowering speed, the rains began. The breezes suddenly turned into gusts, hurling raindrops in different directions. Sheets of rain twisted like swarms of insects or schools of fish. The drops grew huge, pounding the roof with terrible noise. With each wind change, the storm reenergized, strengthened. A peach limb cracked sharply through the din; its fruit was lost.

Distant thunder rolled across the valley and a giant flash illuminated the entire sky. Intense cracks of thunder shook the house. Another flash of lightning was followed by a pause that enveloped me in a brief silence before thunder again rang in my ears. The hail slashed peaches, sliced grapes. The air grew thick with rain, waves leaping back into the air as soon as they hit the ground, meeting the rain sheeting down, like the base of a waterfall.

Then hail began to fall, first with an occasional pellet bouncing off the ground. But larger hailstones soon tumbled to earth, like a cascade of rocks falling down a mountain.

The sky darkened even further, as if night had fallen early. I sensed a god's power, a biblical plague, the wrath of nature. Each stone smashed my harvest, razor edges slitting the flesh. The fruit bled.

The air turned green from the pummeling of leaves and vines. Pounding, thrumming rain. Savage winds. The hail with a tempo, a rhythm beating faster and faster until it was deafening, pulsating, a sustained crash. My harvest was doomed.

Within fifteen minutes, as quickly as it had begun, the storm passed. Rain continued to drip from the trees. The ground was white with ice.

Sunlight peeked through as the sky cleared. To the east the blackness marched toward my neighbors, the horizon darkened from heaven to earth. The hail was now beating another farmer, the same drama to be repeated over and over at other farms.

I inspected the damage. Shredded leaves blanketed the earth. The grapes had turned brown, their berries slit open, guts oozing out. Peach skins were cracked, already infected and gray; rot had settled in.

I drove over to the other side of the farm to visit with Dad. He was sweeping hail out of his shed. "Can you believe that storm?" I blurted.

He looked at me. "It's never hailed like this in June." His eyes scanned his fields. He blinked, then shook his head. "Never," he whispered.

This hailstorm became a story we shared together. We both stopped and looked out into the fields. I took a deep breath, sharing the disaster with my father.

Chapter Eight

LEARNING TO LEAN, WALKING ON UNEVEN GROUND

DAD RARELY PUT himself first. The farm always seemed more important, and running it required confidence. Now he needs to realign that confidence, put himself before anything else.

Relearning a skill that was once second nature is among life's hardest challenges. As if you'd flunked a class, you have to practice activities that you basically know but have trouble doing smoothly. The rest of the world moves on while you are held back, "slow," or at least slowed.

After moving to the rehabilitation center in Fresno, Dad has to work harder than ever to relearn how to stand, how to use his still-compromised right hand, as well as how to see through a fog that seems to cloud his thoughts at times.

Dad wants to walk again. Walking represents independence, freedom, and the opportunity to go home, back to the land. Walking means work. Work completes Dad.

Recovering from a stroke, however, demands patience as well as a fierce drive. Waking up from the stroke seems easy; recovery is the hard part. You acknowledge the losses and respond, retraining yourself to accomplish everyday, once-simple tasks: holding a spoon or pencil, rolling upright to get out of bed, feeling and using your right foot. You are challenged every day and every moment. Most people are unaccustomed to constant physical challenges such as these. Even for a farmer like Dad, who faced intensely physical daily challenges for over six decades, it is difficult.

Initially, Dad's recovery is to be founded on aggressive behavior: attack the deficit in order to renew himself. The more he pushes himself to correct and perfect movement, the faster his therapy will take hold. Yet until now, aggression had not been a part of Dad's character; it didn't belong in his formula for farming. Reserved, almost passive, Dad always confronts a problem thoughtfully. He thinks about things for a long time and embodies a natural ambivalence; his decision was often no decision.

For instance, once we had a bad outbreak of mildew on our grapes. The white fungus coated berries with a fine powder, sucking life from the skin and hardening the surface, which caused the flesh to crack and then rot. Dad called neighbors, talked with a pest control advisor who worked for a pesticide company, conferred with the uncles at family gatherings. He amassed a wealth of knowledge but then decided not to act on the advice he received.

"Split the difference," he'd often say. He decided to wash the mildew off the worst sections, about twenty acres out of our fifty, before it created bigger problems. He hooked up our 500-gallon sprayer and drove through the fields, up and down rows, showering the diseased vines with water, just water, lots of water, almost a gallon per vine.

When I asked about the remaining thirty acres, he claimed they were different. "But why take a risk?" I asked. We talked of using fungicides, even a less toxic, natural one, but he was stubborn. I felt as if I were trying to push a rope. Hesitant to throw a quick fix at a problem, Dad resisted my pleas, unwilling to spend energy and resources on an unproven method. He'd wait to see if the water worked, then think some more.

There's a Japanese term: *gaman*—the will to keep trying over and over, to persevere, to endure. In Japanese culture, *gaman* is one of the most highly valued attributes, honored in those who are dedicated to effort. At that point with the mildew, however, I could not see much difference between perseverance and stubbornness, tenacity and detachment. But perhaps *gaman* also requires an acceptance of life that I could not then see. Certainly, Dad has *gaman*. After all, that innate drive, that strong will got him home even as the stroke was doing its initial damage.

"Pick up your foot."

"Heel to toe, heel-to-toe strides."

"Lift your knee to pull up your foot."

"Don't forget to bend your knee."

Dad remains at the rehabilitation center for weeks. The whole family becomes his support team. We cheer and try to lead with enthusiasm, hoping he feeds off our energies and optimism. We help coach him through his sessions with all the specialists and their treatments, help him overcome the little things that can sometimes overwhelm a steady recovery.

His right foot still drags; he sometimes forgets that it's not working. "Pay attention and focus." "Repeat and practice." "You have limitations, yes, but great progress and promise."

Dad tackles all these steps, is committed to getting better. Grateful for little accomplishments, he—and we—practice balancing expectations with realism.

"Remember, keep your foot in line."

"Don't get lazy and swing your leg out wildly."

"Learn to walk straight."

As he works on this new way of walking, Dad also has to depend on others, which is odd for him. Many other men struggle against leaning on someone else, physically and emotionally, and metaphorically. It's hard for them to listen to others and take corrections in what they're doing, hard to trust others as they had learned to trust themselves. Like Dad, they are used to self-sufficiency. For decades, he and he alone had been responsible for the success and failure of the farm. He liked it that way and was content when working by himself, finding a tranquillity that eludes me. He's happy alone in his fields.

At times, Dad struggles to comprehend all the activity around him at the rehab center. His brain, as well as his body, is still recovering, adjusting to the loss of speech, finding and rerouting neural pathways of understanding to try to reconnect, seek new conduits to compensate for the damage. Therapy helps build those connections as the patient attempts to regain lost skills. Since farmwork gives Dad his identity, the faster we can get him back to the farm, the faster he will heal. We are racing an invisible clock, a timeline of recovery, having been told that what doesn't come back soon is probably lost forever.

As a second son, Dad was used to putting himself second, subordinating his own needs to those of others. Even when he came to be in charge of his parents and teenage siblings, however, Dad did not always stand up for himself. In the past, he may have chosen the path of least resistance. Initially, Dad seemed slow to accept assistance after the stroke. But that changes when he starts physical therapy. He asserts himself, seeks help from others as he relearns how to stand, walk, and turn. I begin to work with him in between the therapy sessions, pushing him to complete additional exercises. He feels my urgency. With a physical injury, people can compensate, find other ways to get things done, although some simply give up and live with it. I don't want Dad to give up. He works to get better. We both need him to return to the farm.

"Remember to bend your knee with each step."

"Heel to toe, heel to toe."

"Pay attention, you have to think constantly about walking."

We enter a slow world, parallel to our fast-paced, high-tech, digital world, where Dad has to relearn how to walk. Farming, too, has always been a slower world, our sustainable practices seemingly out of sync with those of larger farms, walking the fields obsolete for many of today's industrial-scale farmers. Perhaps to my father slow is right, while fast is insulting. He has never moved too fast to think, never raced through thoughts in order to make a decision. He reflects and keeps the world in focus while others rush, blinded by speed.

Dad slowly passes signposts of success: The first assisted step, then one by himself. A stroll down a hall, with no handrail! Up an incline, around the room. He hesitates at the stairs, raising a foot then missing the step—suddenly, we see a new barrier to overcome, a new skill to learn. Nonetheless, Dad grows stronger. He gains confidence as he regains his balance and a sense of his abilities. We as a family grow, too, as we work with him, accepting his new limitations, allowing ourselves to help one another.

Even in this slower world, however, I struggle with the chaos of the healing process. I want a more linear progression and clearer expectations of what's to come. I want even more visible measurements of recovery. To push Dad to get to the next step. Coach him to work harder.

Yet Dad remains a farmer. He takes a few steps forward, pauses and rests, then a few more steps. He's cautious in the face of nature's unknown influences, hesitant to return to the life still awaiting him. One day, he even takes a step backward, satisfied that he has accomplished one more day of work even if he has not made visible outer progress. He seems to accept this chaos and nonlinear progression, the inconsistencies of recovery, healing like a farmer. I worry about who's in control, Dad or the damage from his stroke. I, too, need to learn a new balance, a combination of acceptance and perseverance in my own life and in my approach to farming.

In life, as in recovery, not all things are level and smooth.

"Dad has to learn how to walk on dirt," I announce to his doctor and team of therapists. They stare at me, initially puzzled. "There are no sidewalks out on the farm," I explain.

Dad has to learn how to walk on uneven ground. If he can't walk on dirt, I'm not sure he'll want to come home. Perhaps this is the source of the ambivalence we sense from him. He has to touch the earth and reconnect with his farm: that is what makes him feel real. Dad needs to find out for himself if he can he handle irregular surfaces, learn to feel more through his soles, combine sight and touch so they work together, responding to the irregular terrain. He has to discover where he is.

At first we have difficulty even finding dirt on the manicured hospital grounds; the evenly mowed grass has only a few smoothly raked spots of brown soil. If Dad wants to get back to work, he will have to navigate the roughest territory: soft and hard earth, rocks and dirt clods, rises and dips, shadows hiding divots and holes. Toss in some vine clippings and tree branches, and mud and dust with big clumps of weeds—yes, don't forget the weeds.

Having mastered flat surfaces, Dad needs to find the will to face another challenge and, initially, risk more failure than success. This is hard work, some days better than others. It's not a war with conquests and downfalls or a game with winners and losers. We celebrate little things, accept setbacks. Seek options and make choices that ensure there's another day. The process of healing is actually never completely done—like farming, we will always have more trees and vines to prune, water, and fertilize, always another harvest to pick. A Zen Buddhist phrase comes to mind: "The pot is always boiling." There will always be more uneven ground. It's all natural.

As we challenge Dad to work more, I keep trying to be realistic and to allow him to reach an acceptance stage of recovery, when we will all be satisfied with what we have accomplished. Take one step at a time, then just one more step. Do not lower expectations, but create different expectations. Reinvent yourself because you are now different. Create a ritual, habits of the heart, that form a familiar, secure atmosphere, a structure that purges the negatives. As when farming, learn by observation, osmosis. Let the land provide the learning environment and allow yourself to practice stumbling and recovering with grace. It's the journey that counts, not just the end.

After his stroke, unfortunately, Dad can't be fixed. No pill or surgery or healing technology can reverse the damage completely. Recovery is neither fun nor simple, so we allow him a few moments of self-pity, some time to rest, and then get back out to practice more.

We learn to walk as best we can, wherever we are. We'd all be better off, and become better people, if we had to relearn the little, important things periodically and learn to accept the diverse terrains we have to negotiate. We can all benefit from learning how to walk on uneven ground.

Chapter Nine

SHOVELING SAND

YOU CAN'T TELL someone how to shovel weeds. The best you can do is demonstrate how you do it, then wait. Either the weeds will take over or you'll learn how to keep up with them season after season, much like shoveling sand.

The stroke stripped Dad of some of his confidence. Walking and working the land he called home for fifty years has always defined him; after the stroke, Dad isn't quite sure who he is, even after we get him home. We don't know whether he will become strong enough to prune the vines and orchards or stack brush and burn dead limbs. We worry that, if he resumes his job of checking the irrigation water, he'll grow confused as he tries to calculate how much longer until a row is filled with water, or determine which irrigation valves need to be opened slightly or a lot or shut off completely. So for now, he shovels weeds from around the base of the peach trees. With weeds, he can set his own pace, with no machinery other than a simple shovel involved. To find out what he can do, he basically tests his skills until he stumbles.

Because Dad has shoveled weeds for decades and countless hours, his memory of shoveling will reconnect him to himself and the land, but ironically it could also hinder his recovery by blocking his openness to learning a new method or a modified technique. I can't reteach Dad how to shovel. We will have to reconnect in a new way and allow his brain to mend and rewire itself. Dad is not a machine that we can duct-tape or fasten together with baling wire for a quick fix. Some parts of him will take more time than others to heal and grow again.

When he sees his favorite shovel again for the first time in months, Dad first gently takes it in his hands and holds it, stroking the smooth wooden handle. It's familiar to his hands, comforting to touch. Yet it must also feel odd, alien to his damaged right hand. He now has to train his left hand to do the work the right once did, to guide the shovel blade into the earth and push the steel through the dirt. Although his good left hand and arm still have some strength and dexterity, his dominant hand is now limited to a supporting role, pushing and sometimes slipping off the handle as if it's an understudy who has forgotten his cue.

Dad tries to jab the dirt, targeting a small chickweed. He misses completely, the shovel almost flying out of his hands. He shakes his head, tries again, this time cutting too deep; the blade digs deep into the earth and sticks, a foot short of the target. Shoveling weeds does involve some precision.

I reposition his hands, dropping them farther down the handle, creating a different angle, like choking up on a baseball bat for more control. It works. He slices into the spring earth, chopping the weed at its roots. He grins and seems excited. But next time, his right hand slips off the end, putting an abrupt stop to work again. The right hand just doesn't pay attention, resists reprogramming, wants to work independently. I reposition the hand, lightly slap it twice as if to wake up the nerves. Dad grunts and agrees with the reprimand. He growls, as if to admonish his right hand, warning it to wake up and pay attention.

When I was young, Dad didn't teach me how to shovel, but briefly showed me his method, then left my brother and me to tackle a couple hundred trees over one spring break. Years later, after hundreds of hours of training, I believe I have finally got the hang of it—the secret weapon: education by repetition.

In spite of its awkwardness, shoveling welcomes Dad home. Slicing weeds, clearing grass, leveling dirt is a return to what he knows best and does best. Now he can practice working and reclaiming himself; shoveling also allows for mistakes—you simply do it again.

I step away, removing myself. There can be no master-student relationship here. I show him a few things, step back, observe, help make adjustments. I participate in his recovery, but the majority of the work is his. I once heard a basketball coach say, "The best I can hope for is that by the end of the fourth quarter, we have the opportunity to win." All I hope to do is help give Dad the opportunity for success.

Concentrating, Dad loses himself in the shoveling. Moving with a new rhythm that he has not had since his stroke, he dances with weeds. Oblivious to my presence, he is deep into a meditation with his shovel, weeds, and then no weeds.

When he pauses, he strikes a classic pose, a farmer leaning against his shovel. He pushes his hat back to wipe sweat from his brow and peers over his land. Lean on something, depend on it to hold you up; you can't stand alone, but you have to trust yourself and practice leaning. We share a moment, a passion for the land and a type of compassion for each weed. The weeds have given Dad a new meaning. His shovel glistens in the sun.

An hour later, I check back with him. He has shuffled from one tree to another and another, clearing chickweed and the early spouts of stinging nettle (which we always call "itchy grass"). Dad's shirt is wet from sweat; he has blisters on both palms. But he doesn't want to stop and points to the next tree and a truly evil weed: Johnson grass.

Many shovels have been sacrificed during our epic battles with Johnson grass. Our farm has a tomb of the unknown shovels, a rusting pile that is beyond repair, their handles broken, steel necks of the blades so badly bent by this immovable force that they're unusable. Some blades have worn badly and are no longer able to cut no matter how we try to file and sharpen their edges. Even a few newer shovels have joined the pile, the angle of the blade never quite right for the fight against this beast.

Weeds are public displays of what a farmer can't overcome. Although he came to terms with not being able to eliminate them entirely, they bother him. With Johnson grass, however, he has discovered a purpose for himself that will occupy many days. He will keep shoveling, as the farm needs his help to contain this menace.

I imagine the conversations Dad and I would have with the infamous Mr. Johnson—for whom this weed is named. Perhaps it would be a letter—from farmer to farmer about the trials we have with this weed.

Dear Mr. Johnson,

My father and I have a couple simple questions: Did you imagine when you planted this lush-growing sorghum plant on your Alabama plantation in 1843 that it could spread throughout the land? Did you have an inkling that your legacy would be one of the most noxious, hideous weeds that farmers have to face, forever attached to your name? Farmers and gardeners curse you when it infests a vegetable plot, row crop, vineyard, or orchard. In one of the few times my father has ever sworn, he included your name: "Damned Johnson grass!" Perhaps you had an idyllic vision, but it has become a nightmare from which there's no waking up.

Perhaps you thought that the seeds you acquired from Africa or the Middle East would grow into feed for your cattle, the perfect ground cover for your lands, a high-producing, desirable perennial grass. But the normally palatable forage becomes poisonous to livestock whenever its normal growth is interrupted by drought or frost. You saw a nice patch of tall grass gracefully growing and swaying in the wind, but you couldn't measure the toxic accumulation of hydrocyanic acid in the surviving roots. Still, what were you, nuts?

Hadn't you heard that Governor Means of South Carolina had already experimented with this monster a decade earlier? He had written: "The big grass inspired terror and no one will look at my place." He could not sell his plantation after it was infected with this weed. Yet you thought you could do as you pleased with your property, and with a southern aristocrat's arrogance, you sowed the fertile bottomlands of the Alabama River with pestilence. During the Civil War, cavalry horses ate the lush grass and spread the seeds throughout the South. In the late 1800s, your seeds contaminated the rest of the country when members of Congress annually passed out hundreds of thousands of free grass seed samples and when the United States Department of Agriculture distributed more than 1 million seed samples per year, all contaminated with the seeds of Johnson grass.

I can imagine that my grandfather, a poor immigrant from Japan, felt honored to get a free seed packet from the U.S. government. He would have dutifully sowed the sample in the valley, helping also to plant our family in American soil. Little did he know he may have planted the seeds of a struggling farmer's destruction. In an ironic twist of fate, those seeds also created the demand for a cheap labor supply, immigrants from Japan and Asia, then Mexico, strong backs needed to purge our valley of this scourge.

A single plant of Johnson grass can produce more than five thousand seeds annually, and these seeds can lie dormant in the ground for twenty years. Chop the stalks and new shoots will vigorously push up from the roots in the earth. We can't even burn Johnson grass, because it seems to thrive on that cleansing and easily outcompetes anything else with regrowth.

The plant's secret weapon is its underground stems, rhi-

zomes. From each segment of rhizome, new shoots rise as if from the mythic Hydra. Cut off the head and two will appear. Slice the rhizomes into small pieces and each will regenerate its own plant. Disking and cultivating help them spread even more, as the plant delightedly invades any disturbed ground.

The plant grows dense, up to eight feet tall, easily monopolizing sunlight and crowding out any other growth. Its roots are an immovable force: try to shovel them and your blade will be stopped cold when it strikes the contorted root mass of thick rhizomes, a massive tangled underground ball. The roots we miss produce a natural toxin that prevents other plants from growing close to it. Johnson grass does not make a good neighbor.

How foolish you and others were, thinking you could control nature, import something for your own use, believing only good would come from the innocent-looking reddish seeds. You had heard stories of this grass generating more than two tons of forage with each cutting, and you wanted to produce more and more to create a limitless fortune for yourself and other landowners. Instead, your biological Ponzi scheme cursed a nation.

Some have claimed that your grass would not be that bad were it not so aggressive. Swine apparently relish the roots. Cut for hay, it is nutritious (so long as, prior to cutting, the plant is not stressed so that it produces natural toxins). Some seed dealers today actually sell Johnson grass seeds, but neither my father nor I would call them friends.

While yanking out your grass from our vineyards, many times I have slit my fingers on the razor-sharp leaves. My grandmother called your weed abunai kusa*: "dangerous grass." Unchecked, it will strangle a farm and the farmer, steal water from trees, shade grapes from the sun, overpower a vineyard, and strike terror in a harvest worker. Calling it invasive is an understatement. Both my father and I have awakened from nightmares of Johnson grass sweeping across our valley,* *marching like an army, destroying acres and acres of land. Men and women wage war on it all year, cutting down the stalks and preventing their green growth from surviving, but the roots lie quiet in the earth beneath them, waiting until the people are exhausted, then resprouting with vengeance. Johnson grass is poison for a family farm.*

Your legacy has bankrupted scores of farmers. During western range wars, when neighbors were pitted against neighbor, free-range ranchers against farmers, your seeds of destruction were carried in the bowels of cattle. During a bitter divorce, a rancher claimed that his father-in-law hated him so much that he had helped Johnson grass to become established on his ranch.

I am overmatched by Johnson grass, embarrassed that I cannot clear the land of most of it as my father had largely done. But because I learned of this weed as a youngster and witnessed my father's struggles, I do not interpret my defeat as a huge failure. Your weed is very democratic—it frustrated my father and his father as well as the women in the Masumoto family. My father would come home exhausted after his heroic battles only to march out again the next morning, taking on an enemy we can never completely roust from every corner of our land. Your weed sows humility.

Perhaps you actually had known about the weed's noxious qualities and had visions of profits beyond its foliage potential, since I've read that your family may have had a patent on the French plow. A complicated piece of equipment, a French plow can reach under a grapevine to scoop out a mass of earth that includes Johnson grass and most of its roots—without hurting the vine. The plow does well but is not perfect against this perfect enemy. Today, other farmers are in thrall to Monsanto, the company that invented Roundup, an herbicide that is absorbed into Johnson grass and will kill most of it, although with heavy infestations, they have to reapply the chemical to kill all the rhizomes.

Just as you introduced your folly, envisioning enormous stockpiles of feed and wealth, today scientists have made some crops genetically resistant to Roundup so that farmers can liberally spray the chemical to kill weeds such as Johnson grass but not harm crops—envisioning larger harvests. Yet, already, after only a few years, weeds have found a way to survive. Some, like mare's tail, a tall, skinny summer annual that can grow to over ten feet, are growing resistant to Roundup. So Johnson grass has promoted the proliferation of other weeds.

We would call your grass a plague, but that would imply a cure. It is a curse, something we must learn to live with. We have to accept Johnson's weed's curse, but we will continue to battle it on our organic farm.

With disdain,
The Masumoto Family Farm

Over time, we do make a difference with our shovels, leaving small marks on the land with each stroke-and-pass through the dirt as we recycle our weeds with these shovels, turning their green growth upside down and back into the soil to compost. The weeds infuse dead earth with nutrients that make it alive. Our shovels are themselves marked by the land and weeds; they wear the scars of battle with Johnson grass, which engraves them with the timeline of our family on the land. The hours and hours of labor of one generation slowly abrade the metal from a favorite blade. Dad and I will be outlived by that grass but not destroyed or conquered. We have learned just to hold the handle tighter.

My grandparents had a shovel that was worn down over the decades into a perfect shape for our sandy loam soils. They passed it on to my father and mother, and Dad has left his own mark on it by wearing it down another few inches. Now it is half a shovel, its metal honed to an inward-crescent shape that awaits my own mark.

Chapter Ten

BACK IN THE SADDLE AGAIN

DAD'S NOT WHOLE when he returns home, his right side—including his arm, hand, and leg—still injured. But he's overjoyed to be back on his land and out in the fields. His world has now changed and the old farmer has to learn how to farm again.

When the doctors let Dad out of rehab, they warned us to be careful and to keep an eye on him. "He's not stable and may stumble and fall," they said. "And keep him away from anything dangerous."

Like things on a farm?

"Yes."

Farm equipment?

"Absolutely."

A tractor?

"Positively."

As Dad weeds, his shovel creates a rhythmic cadence scraping against the hardening earth, slicing beneath the surface, the blade rubbing against the sandy loam, severing roots.

After he's been back a week, I walk up to Dad and whisper: "Hey, want to try something? Let's see if you can get up on the tractor."

He immediately grins, sets down his shovel, and shuffles to the back of the shed at a quicker pace than usual, his stride directed and determined. He's excited, and I suddenly worry about the potential failure.

Ever since his return to the farm, whenever I have been doing tractor work, Dad has watched me. I couldn't help but think about how self-conscious I'd been under Dad's watchful eyes when I first came back to the farm twenty-one years before. I'd felt that he was examining my work as I took over the farm, judging my abilities when I tried different things. I wondered if he privately shook his head at my organic farming methods and philosophy of working with nature instead of against her, but I sensed that he agreed with my approach even though he worried about the business of farming without chemicals—the potential loss of productivity, the fruit that would have some cosmetic defects that could result in lower prices, an outbreak of disease or pests that could not be easily controlled with organic treatments. But he simply may have been happy because someone was farming the family land.

Yet now I study him—the old man working before me. He has been transformed from the strongest seventy-something-year-old I knew, with his lean muscles and strong back, to an old man. His stamina is low. Even while resting, his chest rises and falls noticeably, his breathing labored. Pausing from digging weeds, resting both hands atop the shovel handle, he leans his body against his shovel and studies the work he has accomplished and what remains to be done. He leans and watches me become the farmer. On the other hand, perhaps he simply longed to get up on a tractor again.

I'll admit that I had thought about it and for that reason had parked our Massey 135 diesel behind the shed. An "orchard model," this tractor is designed to sit lower to the ground and to pass under low-hanging peach limbs. One of our favorites, this was also the first diesel Dad bought in the 1970s. The steering has lots of play in it, the engine has a tough time turning over, especially in the cold and foggy winter months, and the body and fenders have their share of dings and dents. But the clutch is still tight and the motor, once it starts, sounds fine as it sits in neutral—making a pounding diesel sound, a chopping noise, as if eager to get to work. It still carries power.

Although no one else is home, I feel as if Dad and I have to sneak around, concealing our motives and secretly carrying out our plans.

I glance around, fearing I might see the ghost of a doctor or physical therapist shaking his head as we ignore directives and risk a major accident. I know that when Mom and my sister, Shirley, come home, I'll catch hell. But I believe Dad knows exactly what we are doing and he believes that it's worth the risk.

Mom and Shirley had left for shopping, one of their first trips away from home since Dad had returned. Mom had hovered over Dad for the last few days, adapting to her new role as caregiver. The transition has to be difficult, Dad the traditional male provider, Mom now in charge, caring for Dad.

In the past, their roles have had a few different twists. The lousy prices of peaches and nectarines in the 1960s compelled Mom to work off the farm. She began as a clerk/typist with the USDA and retired with full pension and benefits. Dad, while fitting many typical roles as the head of the household, made few demands, allowing all of us to grow without lectures or challenges. He never yelled at me; I can't remember him overruling any major decision. He pretty much let me grow up the way I wanted—we all had the full freedom of choice, right or wrong.

Now I feel acutely that Dad doesn't have many choices, and I want to try to give him more. Because he is injured, he has had to accept our help and does not resist our efforts. We all adapt to new roles, often unsure of the extent of assistance that Dad needs or requires or even wants. At the beginning of his recovery, we all touched him a lot, because he needed a lot of physical help. In the hospital we helped turn him, lift him, hold him. As he gradually regained his strength, we guided his motions, redirected missteps, partnered in his exercises. We supported him, held gait belts, clutched his arms to help him maintain his balance. Touch helped heal this man. I have hugged him more in these past few weeks than in my entire life. And I never saw Mom and Dad touch so frequently before.

After a week with him home, Mom has begun to relax and they are slipping into a routine. She still refuses to let him be alone, and when she left today said, with a threatening look in her eyes, "You keep an eye on him." As if this tiny, five-foot grandmotherly woman could unleash anything more than a scolding. "Make sure he doesn't try to do too much."

I wait for her to shake an index finger at me, but she passes this time. (Although my children will never forget when their grandmother playfully socked me—after she discovered that at forty-something, her son had had one ear pierced in order to wear a small earring). Yet as she walked into the yard toward the car where my sister waited in the driver's seat, Mom waved to Dad and did shake her index finger at him, "Now, you be careful, hon."

Dad grinned, leaning against his shovel, and nodded obediently.

"And don't let him work too long," she instructed me.

I, too, grin, then nod obediently just like Dad.

Mom frowned just for an instant, then stepped into the car. She was looking forward to a few hours on her own time.

The 135 Massey tractor sits waiting behind the shed to be reunited with her farmer. Dad takes a position on the right side and tries to lift his right foot up onto the running board. He misses twice, but on a third attempt it lands with a thud. I stand to his side, anticipating that, when he pushes up with his left foot and uses the steering wheel as a handhold to pull himself up, I'll have to help by shoving him from behind.

We sigh. "Uhhhhh."

We grunt. "Yoshhhh."

I only need to lift him slightly. He's pleased that he can do most of this himself, another accomplishment in his recovery.

Perched on the running board, he breathes deeply. But the next step is tricky, requiring dexterity and balance. Dad has to kick his left leg up over the belly of the tractor, guiding the limb past the gearshift knobs, avoiding the clutch pedal in order to land with solid footing. I then realize we are on the wrong side; he'll have to support himself with his weakened right leg as the left swings over to the other side.

Too late to start over, so I try to hold him steady. He lifts, swings, and plants his feet, straddling the machine. Dad breathes heavily now, his chest rising up and down—from the physical exertion and excitement of getting up again. I am relieved.

Then he simply sits down as he has done thousands of times before. The air swooshes from the cushion as he sinks into his throne, thrilled, satisfied. He's sweating, almost shaking. He takes off his old straw hat and wipes his brow with his shirtsleeve. I feel we have reached a goal. Dad can climb aboard a tractor. Suddenly, a world of work opportunities opens. We are happy.

Now what? When learning to drive, the hardest part is clutching, starting the engine, and the first movement forward.

I'm standing on the running board on the left side, my feet scrunched to one side, avoiding the clutch and Dad's foot. I lean against the fender, standing above Dad, like an instructor towering over his student. From this vantage point, I can't control the hand throttle (mounted on the right side of dashboard) or the brakes (near Dad's right foot); but the fuel cut-off control is on my side. I figure that's the most important thing to monitor under the circumstances. Besides, I don't anticipate we'll be going that fast. Hell, we can always coast to a stop, and what's the worst thing we'd hit, an old vine or peach tree? We might knock over but not yank out a vine, which I could possibly straighten. If we break a peach limb and have to retrain the rest of the tree to fill the broken gap, the repair will take years but it is replaceable. And it's all worth the ride.

"Let's get started," I instruct. Dad nods. "First, get out of gear, start in neutral." I give him reminders he really doesn't need, but they're helpful for him to hear, nonetheless; guiding him through this once-familiar rite will help him orient himself.

He tries to shift the gear levels with his right hand and misses; his fingers can't grip, his hand flops wildly. It's painful to watch, and I want to do it for him but stop myself—Dad will have to learn for himself.

He gives up on his disobedient right hand and awkwardly reaches over with his left to shift out of gear. Tractors are built for right-handers, so Dad can't exactly tell if he's succeeded in getting into neutral. Most of the time we shift gears by touch, not by sight, and he's not comfortable yet using his left hand, not familiar yet with the signals coming through that side. So he repeats the process, slowly, but necessarily—a tractor won't start while in gear, a safety precaution to prevent accidents, good for beginning drivers and stroke victims.

His left leg is already bearing down on the clutch, a habit from decades of tractor work. Key turns, the starter cranks, engine sputters and coughs, diesel injects into cylinders, ignites, explodes *rat-ta-ta-ta* then churns with a roar. We both instinctively reach to lower the hand throttle. As the engine slows then runs smoothly, Dad smiles.

"Not too fast," I suggest. Dad stares straight ahead, ready to go. "Let's start in first gear, high." Dad reaches down and drops the levers into place, beginning to teach his left hand.

"No need to rush, take it easy." He eases up on the clutch, we gently begin to roll. We have liftoff.

The dirt passes beneath us; we head down one of our many avenues crisscrossing the farm. It takes about thirty seconds to turn down a larger avenue. Dad handles the maneuver well with his left hand; the right one tries but mostly rests on the steering wheel. At least it looks natural as he pretends to drive with both hands.

We move forward, slow and steady. "Dad, this is great!" I'm content with the test, the experiment, and grow comfortable with the risk, feeling more responsible for this challenge.

We continue down the dirt lane, shifting and swaying with the uneven surface. It feels strange still to be hovering over my father. Dad reaches over, revs the engine, the motor increases RPMs, a slight delay before the bulky machine rumbles forward. We go faster then slower, faster then slower. He's playing.

I think about stopping because we have accomplished so much, learning what Dad can and can't do, enough for one day's lesson. I begin to believe that Dad agrees. He pushes his left leg and engages the clutch, then moves to shift gears. He may want me to take over and take us home, but he doesn't ask. (Of course I forget: he can't ask, having lost his voice with the stroke.)

Dad smoothly shifts from first gear into fourth, pops the clutch, and holds on. We leap forward with a jolt that flings our heads backward. I grab at the fender to catch myself from flying off the tractor.

"Whoa, Dad, take it easy."

He, too, was caught off guard by the launch. His fingers clutch the steering wheel so tightly his knuckles turn white.

"Not too fast, Pops."

I try to recover and reach over to suspend my hand over his, ready to correct his steering gently.

"No rush, Dad."

But Dad now has the look of pleasure as the earth races under us, the rows of vineyards passing like frames of a movie. We roar down the avenue, the wind in our faces, the air streaming across our cheeks, slicing through our hair. We bounce over the uneven trail. I have to admit, I feel the rush of excitement with the speed. Dangerous but thrilling, almost out of control. Too fast. Right on the edge. Feeling young.

Even so, I worry about hitting something in the road, which is a little foolish: Dad and I have memorized this dirt avenue, having passed over her rough surface three or four times a day, easily a thousand times a year. In my life on the farm, could that total over thirty thousand times? And Dad—fifty thousand passes? We know almost every pothole and mound, and I anticipate all the nuances, preparing myself with an anatomical response: my butt cheeks tighten unconsciously as we approach a bump. We can ride out the rough spots. They are not an issue.

Now we're zipping along at four miles per hour. It feels so much faster out in the open air, sort of like riding a motorcycle. Because Dad needs to learn to trust himself—and we need to learn to trust him—I let us go on.

Dad looks happy, taps the throttle, and we surge forward even faster.

"Slow down, slow down."

He keeps pace.

"I think we're going too fast," I yell.

We strike a small pothole and the front left tire dips, then is launched off the ground just for a moment. We whip to the left, Dad jerks the steering wheel to correct, we swerve to the right before straightening out.

"You okay? Are we okay?"

Dad just grins.

Behind us the dust is kicking up, leaving a trail, showing the world how fast we're going. If Mom drives by and sees this telltale evidence, she'll be upset.

"Let's take it easy, Pops."

I reach down and pull the throttle, a gentle reprimand for going too fast. For a moment Dad frowns like a child who didn't get his way, but his disappointment quickly evaporates, and he smiles again as we bounce down the dusty trail.

Slower now, an even pace. I lean against the fender and sense something familiar. I've been here before—thirty years ago when Dad taught me how to drive a tractor, standing next to me, warning me to go slow, allowing me to steer myself, to make mistakes and learn. I was proud of myself then, and now I'm proud of Dad.

This is where Dad belongs. On one side stand the orchards we planted together; some trees more than thirty years old, an ancient old-growth forest by peach-tree standards. Nearby, a ninety-year-old vineyard stretches out, the oldest living things here. Ahead sits another vineyard Dad carved out of hardpan soil: the vines he started the year my grandfather died from his stroke as he was cleaning rootstocks for Dad to plant. These places have meaning, an anthology of stories. They are part of the anatomy of our family farm.

Like an old cowboy thrown from his horse, Dad has gotten back in the saddle again. To work. To feel alive. To be part of something. Dad had taught me all he could, and now it was my turn to give back. As the breeze strokes our faces, Dad looks forward watchfully, but his hands are now relaxed as he steers. I can hear his voice again through his smile.

Part Three

Farm Works

Chapter Eleven

SEASON OF DIRT

SPRING OFFERS A reprieve from the cold, short days of winter. I log long hours in the fields, renewing myself by working outdoors; all my senses seem to awaken with the change in weather. I connect with old friends: shovels, rakes, trowels, snipping shears that have sat quietly in the corner of the shed all winter, ignored and forgotten. I justify my neglect by believing that they, like the plants they tend, must hibernate and rest, waiting out the cold, trusting that, following harsh winters, spring will come.

I run my hands over the handles of the old farm tools, wiping off the fine layer of dust that has collected, stirring them up for work. I add a drop of oil to the pruning shears, lubricating the pivot bolt, and then warm us both up: gripping the handles, I pump with my arms, opening and closing the cutting blades. Shovels and hoes are different; their metal has browned from the winter fog and moisture and grown a light layer of rust, but they like to be prepped by being immersed in the dirt itself. With a few healthy plunges into the earth, the metal is wiped clean, the gray steel shines, the cutting edges silver and ready.

My emotional attachment to inanimate objects might seem excessive, but I do get passionate about farming—about everything having to do with farming—especially in spring. Dad would never use such language about his tools, but he, too, gets excited at the onset of this season of renewal. He sharpens and smooths his pruning shears' blade, slowly guiding the file across the cutting edge over and over, stopping to examine his work, then starting over. Whenever the handle of a favorite shovel breaks, Dad carefully measures another one, fitting it to match his relatively short height (we're both about five foot six).

Spring awakens our valley, stirring life within flora and fauna. With the sun's warmth on our cheeks, we forget that other places still have snow as well as threats of late spring frosts that stalk fresh, tender young growth. But in our valley, we are fortunate: life starts early.

Farmers and gardeners share this sensitivity to spring's calling. We all long to get outside, breathe in the air and touch the earth with our hands. We want to feel the damp soil under our fingernails, to break winter's crust and its hold on us by turning the earth, freeing a spirit in the land. Growing things seems natural, a distinctly human act, part of our desire to cultivate, grow, and create that can seem out of place in our fast-paced, knowledge economy. Farms and gardens foster natural connections that follow slow timelines, much like learning.

I've often thought that all students and teachers should be required to grow something, so that they can better understand the patience it requires and the long developmental curves. We can all benefit from planting seeds and practicing the patience it takes before we see the flowers bloom. I sometimes fantasize: what if all professions required their members to know how to garden? If businesspeople, lawyers, doctors, and politicians had to pass a gardening test, a personal humility might be fostered as they experienced some humbling harvests.

With spring's calling, we allow the senses back into our lives. One of my Japanese neighbors, a retired farmer, prunes a bonsai pine by feeling the needles with his hands and fingers and skillfully guiding the clipper to the unwanted growth to cut it off. He could prune blindfolded, allowing a touch world to guide him. When I ask him how he knows which branch to cut, he doesn't respond, but simply keeps working. I wait and watch more closely. His hands massage the needles, running his palms over them, suddenly stopping, snipping, and starting his search again. He pauses just for a moment, as if a sixth sense guides him to a specific place to perform a task. His work is like that of a skilled hairdresser. Their movements gentle yet rapid, they feel for the strands that are out of place, trimming to allow the desirable growth to fall back into place, to thrive. They both create a natural appearance, their best work looking as if a craftsperson had never been there.

My neighbor simply shows me by example, much as Dad did when he and I worked over the years. Spring lessons were crucial, as the results of this season's work would be multiplied throughout the rest of the year. I've learned to watch, listen, and pay attention—spring demands that of you.

Nonetheless, as my neighbor prunes his pine, I ask one more time: "How do you know which branch to cut?"

Again, he doesn't answer, but looks up, blinks, and returns to the pine. For an instant, I think he is teaching me a Zen lesson, having me simply pay attention to the moment.

A few seconds pass, then my neighbor looks at me and asks, "Did you say something? I can't hear that well anymore."

He smiles. I say nothing, just smile in return.

Appropriately, Dad returned to the farm in spring. Life awakens with his presence and his touch. He has recovered enough to do light farmwork—shoveling weeds, monitoring the irrigation water, helping with some tractor driving.

Standing in the sunlight, he enjoys the heat, absorbing the warmth, grinning to be here. Today Dad spades the weeds. They, too, are warmed by the sun and seek its life-giving energy. Like Dad, they find comfort in the light. In a synergy between the two, the weeds give work that Dad seeks. Both struggle to belong, both are survivors; neither wants to go away. They seem to need each other, and discover each other again every spring.

After the cold of winter that requires thick jackets and two pairs of socks, I begin to shed my clothes in the spring light, wanting to feel weather with my skin: to recover that tactile relationship. I seek to touch something and be touched in return—like a good hug. Because late winter and early spring sometimes blur together, however, I still seek to insulate myself a little from the cold or heat—it's as if my body believes that life should be lived someplace between sixty-eight and seventy-two degrees. Like many in our modern society, I lose a greater sense of how the world feels for a time every year. My relationship with the land, on the other hand, allows me to reclaim that sense, to remember it, perhaps earlier in the season than people who work indoors.

Even so, I, too, often ignore opportunities for feeling with all my senses—I lose touch with the meaning of touch, as if I've been programmed not to pay attention. For instance, in our great fast-food eating revolution, we have done away with utensils. When we eat with our hands, however, most will not remember the sensation of a sesame seed bun or French fry on our fingertips. If we are unaware of the feel of our food, aren't we also likely to be unaware of the importance of the hands that work to bring us that food? Through our senses we pay attention. When we pay attention, we remember. Our brain cells store our experiences, our lives. Too often, though, we consume with no memory. We ignore our senses and our lives.

In an annual ritual, with my first spring contact with the earth, I stimulate all my senses. My eyes tell me that there is sunlight, less fog, longer days. When I touch the damp earth, I can feel spring. Close up, I can smell something rich in the earth, almost like the fattening aroma of chocolate. In this soil lies the origins of dessert.

Pause and stop to listen. At first I hear only my breathing. I become lost in the thoughts of a garden growing, a farm flush with green: the vegetables, fruits, grapes, and harvest. My mouth waters in anticipation.

Later, like Dad, I spy the first green shoots of weeds, which won't let me forget the work and the sweat to get to those lush harvests. But I also continue to enjoy their color and the moment, for these are not yet weeds, just misplaced plants. All green, the color of spring surrounds me, marking the end of winter.

To begin the spring, I rub my hands together and chant: "This is a season to get dirty."

Chapter Twelve

PERFECT JUNK

LIKE ALL GOOD farms, we have a junk pile. It comes with any farm and its succession of owners. Each farmer and generation contributes to the collection of odd machine parts, old equipment, and discarded history. The pile stays put, planted as if it is part of the landscape, growing with each decade. No one plans to grow a junk pile, but one naturally evolves along with farmers and their history.

Some people are distracted by the randomness and seemingly chaotic pile of the unwanted objects in a junk pile. They say: "Clean it up." "It looks terrible." "What a mess." But Dad has not thrown away a single piece of equipment. Every time he fixed something, he found the perfect piece for the repair in his junk pile. Dad shows me the value that is inherent in junk.

When I first came back to the farm, my major contribution to the pile was to restack most of it onto wood pallets to make it portable. I can now move parts of it from one spot to another, fooling myself and others, pretending to clean it up.

Like a modern archeologist who uses modern machinery to rummage through layers of history, I use the junk to glean new ideas and inspiration as well as to fix old things. When a sculptor friend and

I probed the pile, he grew excited by the variety of odd shapes and angles. We pulled out a bright-orange forked steel tooth from some type of harvester, sat it upright and then on its side, walked around it and looked at it closely. He then buried it in the dirt and called it modern art. I left it in place for a few months, carefully working around this art installation until I needed to cultivate the area, then tossed it back onto the junk pile and called it postmodern art.

In our junk, treasures lie hidden. Old pieces from equipment, often broken, mostly dissected into parts of old parts, tell me stories of our farm. Time is left behind in these layers of relics, but not as fossils are or as memorials to the past are, but as remains that future farmers can also mine and use. (At least, that's what I tell Marcy.)

After I spoke at a farm conference in Wisconsin, an old farmer dressed in overalls approached me to talk about his junk pile. "Out here we don't call them 'junk piles,'" he announced. I thought he was going to use the expression "bone pile," which is rarely heard in California.

Instead, he said, "Out here we call them . . ." He then leaned closer to me, as if whispering a secret. "We call them 'inventory.'"

Every year we have to make changes on the farm. Things break, practices change, we face new demands. Old equipment challenges the small family farmer: we can't afford to buy the new, can't afford to discard the old. So we hold on to the old with great determination. We learn to live with the obsolete without becoming obsolete.

Dad's tractors age comfortably because we make minor repairs regularly, like giving them an annual checkup with the doctor. It can take a decade before I notice something is not working well anymore and is harder to repair. Denial easily plants itself along with crops in farming. When we can't afford major repairs and simply don't think about a looming disaster but distract ourselves, then things do not seem so bad in the present. Blind optimism and hard work have their advantages. They can keep you going till you break through to the other side—of a season or a stroke.

Dealing with slow-growth obsolescence, I learn to get by with most of my equipment, mastering their tricks and tics and personalities to get us through another season. One tractor's transmission sometimes locks up—the gear rings don't slide properly and get me stuck in reverse. I have actually spent an entire day going backward—you simply learn to go slow and see the world through a different lens that tests your patience. After my initial frustration and anger, I had to accept the situation and began to study the trees and vines from a new point of view. I laughed as I brought a smile and wave from my neighbor's workers. After some trial and error, I discovered that I can jimmy the gears loose and unjam the transmission with the proper long screwdriver. My solution to this tractor's decline is to keep an extra screwdriver in the fender toolbox at all times, just in case.

Big farms and wealthy operations don't keep old equipment, but on our farm we consider our aging equipment to be valuable precisely because it is old. Our old tools have become *antiques*—without the pejorative connotation that many assign that term. Perhaps because their pace of life is slower, many old farmers have a passion for their elderly equipment—and a compassion, too. We often rediscover the value of objects as we recycle them.

Old equipment conveys lessons about a time when there were more failures than successes, a time when you tried things and if they didn't work, you tried something else. Modern farming methods aim for instant success: you spray a pest-control treatment or apply fast-acting fertilizer and you expect overnight results. With our old equipment, I work more like an artist than a chemist, striving for a perfect performance that is elusive. This is why I have to keep practicing.

As Dad slowly heals from his stroke, he gradually does more farmwork than spading the weeds. He relearns skills, finding comfortable rhythms with his injured right side, as he works pruning shears and settles into a familiar cadence. He drives those tractors that are easier to climb on, memorizing again the fields with rows that are straight and do not place high demands upon the tractor driver.

I try to modify equipment for him. All tractors have their throttle and hydraulic controls on the right side, but as Dad's hand reaches for these familiar levers, it misses, blindly swinging in the air, groping for something and striking nothing. I manage to weld an extension to the levers so he can reach them with his left hand. He has to lean over and reach across his body to grab the knob. I watch, then modify the adjustment, finding a longer shaft he can readily grab.

I can make a mechanical adjustment, but Dad must adapt to the situation, change the way he works when he encounters a glitch. I ride with him on a tractor. He can easily drop a disc into the dirt using the hydraulic controls or adjust the throttle as we rumble down a row. But getting to the end of the row now poses a problem: he needs a step-by-step lesson on how to pause, lift the disc, turn and drop the blades, a function he used to do without stopping. We devise a strategy and adapt old habits to new protocols. Dad works slowly, stopping at the end of every row, leaning over and pulling the hydraulic control so that the disc rises and frees itself from the earth, then he turns the tractor and drives carefully into another vine row. There he stops, plants the tandem disc, and all is set for one more pass down a new row. Each turn is another small victory for Dad. He and his favorite tractor combat obsolescence together with these accomplishments.

Some equipment bedevils him, however. He simply cannot adapt to operating the forklift, for instance. He understands the movement forward and backward and remembers how to use the shift that dictates direction. But the control for up and down confounds his thinking. He keeps mixing them up; instead of lifting a load, he drops the load or vice versa. Eventually that confusion affects his other senses and compounds his mistakes: He tries to raise a pallet and instead backs up. He knocks over a small pile of boxes. Instead of lowering the load, he jerks the entire forklift forward. The forks crash into another pallet, which sets off a chain reaction of failures.

We practice, but the three dimensions of a forklift are just too complex. He can't get his bearings; he's lost this special orientation. We agree that he should no longer load or unload with the forklift, especially during the summer when fruit is picked and shipped. Sadly, he can't fully participate in the harvest, the culmination of every farmer's year.

It will take time for Dad to trust himself, to relearn the wisdom that still lives inside him, to find new routes back into it and ways to unearth it and put it to use. It will take time for me to learn how to modify, repair, adapt our old equipment from previous generations to the demands of present-day organic farming. I have to discover and rediscover ways to use these remnants of the past, such as the weed cutters and cultivators Dad used before the arrival of herbicides. The time I can take to experiment is limited; economic challenges continue to grow. Farming will not get easier, and I can't do it all. But we've learned that simply working harder and longer isn't enough. I need to broaden my thinking and allow for new, creative approaches to old problems. Dad trusts me—to modify our tools and provide opportunities for him to work. He and his old equipment create a symmetry.

In order to save the past and to preserve our farm in the present, I need to make choices and expand my definition of success. While I dream of growing the perfect peach, I may not need to do everything with machine-like accuracy or efficiency, but rather do it just right enough.

A "just-right" theory of life manifests itself on the farm in two ways: baling wire and duct tape. One of the most useful phrases and activities Dad taught me is "to baling-wire something."

The dictionary doesn't include the verb *to baling-wire*, but it should: "to use old wire for repair jobs." In the past, this remedy was reserved for us farmers, part of a rural and agrarian legacy when commonplace items were used for everyday do-it-yourself repairs. Simple and inexpensive—how more fixes should be today. Only a generation ago, people didn't have the resources to call in a professional. They had to be self-reliant in dealing with problems and breakdowns and in responding to emergencies.

Dad and his generation know exactly what baling wire is all about. This pliant, thin wire used to be wrapped around a bundle of hay in two strategic places; strong enough to keep the straw and fibers intact, yet simple to cut and discard. But old-timers rarely discarded the wire. It was too valuable. Dad kept a small barrel full of baling wires saved from earlier days when our farm had livestock and used hay. He pulled some out whenever a farm emergency demanded a quick repair job. As his stash grew small, he rationed it for the most important uses. With a little time and originality in wrapping, he could baling-wire most anything that was broken and, voilà, it was fixed. Over time, it might loosen, but, since this was supposed to be just a temporary remedy, tolerance levels were broad. And we couldn't beat the price.

With Dad's handiwork, fences were held up with baling wire, shovel blades reconnected to broken handles, even axles fastened to a trailer bed. He wove the flexible wire through a barn wall to hold up a shelf or siding. It also worked almost as well as real hinges for doors and other movable parts. Our family used the wire indoors too, to hang things on walls or hold together a screen door. It could even be employed on furniture, keeping a leg attached and a chair upright, so long as it wasn't bumped too hard.

Dad's old pickups seemed to have an affinity for baling wire, especially the tailgates. When the hinge broke, or when the support arms (or chains on older models) wore out and snapped, or latches no longer wanted to work, baling wire came to the rescue. Old trucks (and especially old tractors) inevitably lost their mufflers, which would break loose, rattling beneath the driver, scraping the dirt with every slight bump in the road. Loose mufflers never heal themselves. (I have tempted fate by letting them dangle until another family member—a watchful father or mother-in-law—would not allow me to drive the vehicle.) Dad's quick twist of baling wire fixed the problem. The wire helped prolong the life of thousands of aging trucks, healing them from overuse and neglect. Baling wire prevents obsolescence.

On old farm equipment, if a bolt or weld snapped, the wire proved its worth, replacing the joint and reconnecting a blade or arm to an A-frame. Because most of our farm implements are old, precision repairs are not usually demanded. Nature doesn't seem to mind if the wire wiggled loose and a plowed row or cultivated field isn't exactly straight. Dad would rationalize: perhaps an uneven row was better; the vines and trees don't seem to mind a crooked furrow.

Whenever baling wire's virtually permanent fixes broke, we could easily and simply "re-baling-wire" them. There is an art to wrapping the wire around a broken spot and a school of thought that more is better. With a plentiful supply of wire, you can simply keep wrapping more and more wire, sometimes in a cross pattern, fixing the break better and better. Why wrap it once or twice when ten times must translate into ten times better? Whenever I would self-consciously fix something with Dad watching, the more nervous I became, the more I wrapped the wire, and the more Dad would nod his head in agreement.

For a century, baling wire was valued. Neighbors would drop by to pick up a supply of the cure-all from the farmer. City relatives would visit country cousins; farms became depositories of a needed community resource. Supplies kept well for years, stored in barns and stashed in toolsheds; always reliable and dependable, a good friend to have around.

Baling wire was a metaphor for farm economics and family finances. Small farms barely held it all together, mending leaking operations by patching them here and there, finding a way to get through another year, another season. We grew accustomed to hanging on and measured value in ways other than money. When using baling wire a lot, you work with humility.

Not many people use baling wire anymore, and the seemingly inexhaustible supply has run out. Hay bales are now tied with twine, a cheap, thin strand of rope, too weak to be reused. Yet with the demise of baling wire, we may have lost a creative spirit. We toss away things rather than fix them, or we tolerate things that have broken, no longer trusting ourselves to find solutions and repair our environments. We increase the stuff that goes into landfills and garbage dumps—junk that can't be used and recycled. People with resources throw money at problems, believing experts can solve things, ignoring simple options or repairs they could attempt themselves.

Duct tape has stepped into the gap left by the demise of baling wire, however, and has renewed my spirit and belief in people and their ability to fix things. That gray, ubiquitous, magical mender is a fitting replacement for baling wire. "To duct-tape something" is my new favorite phrase. I'm part of a duct-tape era. I have a duct-tape farm. I employ the tape in innovative ways from emergency repairs to simple jobs. I'm not alone; duct tape is every handyman's (and -woman's) secret weapon.

Other tapes—Scotch and adhesive tape—don't have the sticking power and strength. Electrical tape can stretch and does not hold well when wet. White adhesive tape for bandages, which comes on a metal spool in a nifty metal case, held allure when I was a child, but it was expensive and too narrow for repair work. Once I wrapped almost an entire spool around a fraying baseball. It worked for only a few pitches and then grew a tail of detached tape that made for a great screwball (when whacked by my brother, it looked like a comet sailing through the air).

Inexpensive, simple, duct tape creates a world of possibilities and enables a quick fix. Its strength comes from the fabric-lined backing, which keeps it from stretching like other tapes. The glue is a sticky sensitive adhesive that, when pressure is applied, marries the adhesive with the surface. The degree of the bond is determined by the amount of pressure used.

With duct tape, I quickly discovered that, the more I messed with it, the better it held. Want something to stick better? Just apply more pressure. Want a stronger fix? Just add more tape. For the not-so-handy, this was magical. No wonder duct tape has been called "Jesus tape"—it can perform miracles.

By some accounts, duct tape originated during World War II as a waterproof sealing tape for ammunition cases. The fabric backing proved easy to rip to fit repairs on military equipment. Later, it was called "hundred-mile-an-hour tape" because it worked in extreme weather conditions, including rains and wind. (NASCAR teams often use duct tape for quick repairs during races.)

Because it resists water, some call it "duck tape," but the name comes from its use on heating and air-conditioning ducts. Ironically, today one of the few things duct tape does not work well on is ducts—the typical, everyday duct tape we buy from the hardware store is now prohibited by building codes in many places, including California.

But on the farm, we have no such prohibitions. Employing Dad's sense of ingenuity, my motto is that a handyman or -woman needs only two tools: duct tape and WD-40 (a penetrating oil that works as a lubricant and anticorrosive solution). Generally, I approach problems with this principle: "If it's stuck, add WD-40. If you want it to stick, use duct tape."

I've used the tape on tractors and trucks, clothes and hats (especially our collection of farmer's archetypal crushed straw hats), seats and cushions, boxes and trays. It keeps rope from fraying, handles from shedding splinters, and gloves with holes in service for just a few more rounds.

I've tested it in organic farming, reversing it to see what insects it could trap, thus monitoring population levels. I've tried using it as a barrier to keep crawling worms and larvae from working their way up a branch. I'll often tag branches with a strip of duct tape and write a note (with a Sharpie, another wonder tool) as my numerous farm experiments unfold.

Other farmers have utilized duct tape as bandages and short-term casts on their animals' legs. It can fasten a cow's tail to her hind leg to keep it out of the milker's eyes. It can hold pins and bolts in place during repair work, creates fasteners for gates and fences, repairs bags and hoses. It extends the life expectancy of work boots.

Nonfarm uses vary widely, from home repairs to fashion design:

duct-tape handbags, dress shirts, and even push-up bras. The company that manufactures Duck Tape sponsors a "Stuck at the Prom" contest in which participants make their prom gowns and suits from Duck Tape, which comes in an explosion of colors. Duct tape has been called the musician's best friend, fixing cases and instruments. Tribute songs include my favorite, "When I'm Stuck, I Turn to Duct Tape." The first lyric begins: "I never had fun with nails, I turn to duct tape."

Perhaps the most famous use of duct tape was in 1970 during the failed *Apollo 13* mission. While en route to the moon, the module lost power and astronauts needed to modify a square carbon dioxide filter so that it could fit into a round receptacle and allow them to breathe and make repairs so they could return to Earth. Engineers redesigned the scrubber in two days using duct tape. Scientist Keith Canfield, who thought of the modification, said later that he knew the problem was solvable when it was confirmed that duct tape was on the spacecraft.

I'm addicted to duct tape. As I follow my just-right theory of life, I don't always have the time, the resources, or the energy for permanent fixes. What can be fixed "permanently," anyhow? Realistically, temporary repairs often turn into long-term solutions and emergency situations demand quick fixes. Since I may not know how to solve a problem correctly, a duct-tape answer fits my limited capacity: I just don't know any better. I find this wonderfully freeing. I admit my shortcomings yet am willing to try something—yes, even duct tape. It's okay not to know everything, just duct-tape it and see what happens.

On the farm, duct tape symbolizes my thinking—both literally and figuratively. I'll walk by something that is duct-taped and grin. Whatever it is, it is doing just fine. My duct-tape remedies are scattered visibly across my farm. It has helped me perfect my junk pile and prevents things from becoming all used up and obsolete. It frees me to tackle the big issues with the right resources, striving to make things better. By enabling a quick fix, it creates opportunities for other work to transition from good to great. By allowing smaller things to be just right, duct tape contributes to my larger quest for perfection.

Duct tape fits a self-reliant culture, a do-it-yourself and can-do attitude. When you use duct tape, you start trusting yourself. We all need just-right, duct-tape solutions. For many of our biggest issues—health care, education—what if all we have, like *Apollo 13*, is duct tape? We have to do our best, accept when just right is good enough, and selectively determine what we can and want to do great.

Obviously, the environmental issues that challenge our Earth require long-term fixes that will need both resources and political will. But while we search for them, we can also find short-term, quick fixes that will require fewer resources and can be accomplished with limited political cooperation. The next generation may want to use superglue for permanent fixes, but a duct-tape solution might be all that's possible for now, the first step in a longer process.

Imagine if politicians could adopt a duct-tape work ethic and be able to admit it whenever they don't have the answer—they could revert to duct-tape solutions, knowing they're not perfect but that at least they're trying. Likewise, perhaps the public will stop condemning leaders for experimenting and acknowledge when duct tape works well enough.

We're in an economic downturn. Money is not easy to come by. To boost economic recovery, perhaps we should send everyone a roll of duct tape to fix things and save money. We might even discover situations for which duct tape works so well that it becomes a permanent solution—not perfect, perhaps, but sustainable.

Now that Dad himself needs continuous repairing, we have committed to our just-right philosophy. Our operation—held together by baling wire and patched up with duct tape—is a metaphor for any kind of recovery. A resourceful farmer never, ever says, "I don't think duct tape will fix it." We persevere. We are farmers.

Dad drives the tractor and occasionally crashes into things, mainly grapevines. I'll discover shreds of a trunk stuck on a disc blade or look down a row and see an old vine askew. I investigate and discover he drove too far to one side and the disc blades hooked a gnarled old vine trunk and its metal stake and ripped them out of the ground. I sometimes find the dead vine carcass lying a few yards away, Dad oblivious to the accident.

Do I tell him? No. We make sacrifices. I learn to live with it and experiment with other, "just-right" solutions. They just might work.

Chapter Thirteen

THE ART OF GOING SLOW—FRENCH PLOWING

CHARACTER IS REVEALED when working with a French plow.

In the 1950s, Dad farmed with a team of mules named Jackie and Molly, who pulled plows, wagons, and cultivators. I imagine Dad as a mule whisperer with his gentle touch and soft way of talking. The mules were very bright, especially about work. When they hauled a French plow to pull dirt and weeds out from under the grapevines, they worked methodically and consistently, trudging down vine row after vine row. When the plow hooked a grapevine, the mules would feel the tension and stop, whereas a tractor and disc will yank the entire plant from the earth. According to Dad, the mules knew to pause to save the vine and, of course, their own energy, refusing to struggle any more than necessary.

"Tractors," Dad said, "don't have that kind of common sense."

I know this is true from my first unfortunate efforts to French plow, which proved that vines are no match for tractors. I'm not as smart as a mule and have pulled out my share of vines over the years.

Spring is French-plow season, when farmers break winter's hold on the land by disking the soil. The smell of freshly opened earth fills the air.

An 1878 report from the Universal Exposition at Paris describes a crude plow that the French used to cultivate their rich vineyards and "keep the soil open and free from weeds." At the heart of the plow was the moldboard, a curved wood or metal blade that digs into the earth and then turns the earth over to one side. As the plow forges ahead, a small furrow is created in its wake. Eventually the French plow was imported, copied, updated, and produced in America. Many grape growers in our valley have a French connection, so a sense of history lives in our French plows.

While reliable, the French plow demands patience—the farmer has to drive slow, real slow. You can walk faster than the pace of French plowing. Even our oldest dogs, hobbling on ancient legs, like to stroll alongside of me while I work with a French plow; I believe they feel young as they match the speed of the tractor, accompanying their owner up and down each row like loyal, obedient guardians.

Before herbicides were invented, the French plow was the tool of choice in vineyards. To dig weeds out and away from grapevines, a plow has to first swing past the trunk, ease back to till directly under the vine trellis and canes, then swing back out again and dodge the next vine. Over time, the device has been modified and redesigned, improved and adjusted. Many vines have been sacrificed in the name of progress, and many modern farmers consider the French plow outdated and obsolete. I want to keep using the French plow, however, because traditional processes interest me. I believe they are valuable, these intersections of human nature and nature with a farm tool mediating between them.

Dad taught me how to French plow years ago with an older machine that was difficult to use, even harder to adjust. Getting it set up was complicated, as was determining the speed of the tractor, the angle of the blade, and the proper depth of the cut. Dad never explained those details, but expected me to figure them out on my own, since the pace and settings he used would only fit his temperament, not mine. For example, Dad anticipated the fact that I like to drive a little faster than he, which affects how the plow spring will retract to avoid a vine trunk (or not), lessons I could determine only after a few days or weeks or even years (and a few accidental removals). He allowed me to discover my own work rhythms.

Rescuing a farming practice isn't quite like writing out directions. There is an art to it, an expression found in the angle and speed of French plow work, the rhythms of the blade leaving a pattern in the earth, and a willingness to practice and learn through trial and error.

While French plowing, it also helps to employ other traits: diligence, tenacity, and a contentment with being alone. Some critics add antisocial attitudes, if not just a willingness to be with plants more than humans and the drive to go in circles all day. I'll spend hours in my vineyards daily, simply going up one side of the vine row, then down the other. The tractor crawls along to allow the plow to dig weeds at only one vine at a time. By the end of a day, having spent hours traversing the relatively small area of a football field, I may look up and calculate that I have completed only a few rows of vines. The trick is then to feel as if I have still made progress.

French plowing hurts my back and neck, which ache from constantly having to look backward to monitor the plow behind the tractor. One false move and the blade could uproot a vine; you get no do-overs with the French plow. Even so, I'm tempted to speed up, push the pace a little, shave a few seconds from each vine. It works for a while, but I'll inevitably hook a big taproot and immediately will be humbled back into first gear, while weeds sneer and grow taller in the warm spring air.

Spending so much time in one place allows me to become comfortable with the land. I learn the nuances of our farm—the sandy spot near the irrigation canal, the heavier clay by the corner of the fields, the lighter-colored earth near the avenue. In this way I become grounded. I inherit Dad's sense of place, an elemental connection with the individuality, the face of our land that will influence any future decisions.

Although I bridle against the slowness, I actually have it lucky because my current plow is equipped with modern hydraulics. All I need to do is to keep it going straight. Older French plows required more agility and focus to drive and steer. Yet even with this newer machine, memory matters: over the years, I have had to become familiar with certain rows that are narrow on one end and wider at the other and to remember which blocks of vines were planted at different ages and are thus gnarled and twisted. In these potential problem areas, simply going straight won't work. I have to swerve around these elderly creatures. Sometimes I long for the experiences that are locked up in Dad's brain, wishing he could simply download them to me.

By perfecting my French plowing techniques I'll complete my trial-and-error learning curve. My progress will be rooted in the history of our land, in what has worked in the past and continues to allow us to work harmoniously with nature in the present.

In our junk pile lie three generations of French plows. One version, mostly in pieces now, was made about the time tractors replaced farm horses and mules and is the plow that Jackie and Molly dragged. Walking behind the team and plow, Dad would grip the handles tightly. As they approached a vine, he had to lean left and twist the two-foot curved blade, swinging the plow around the vine trunk, then quickly lean to the right to drive the blade edge back under the vine trellis—inches away from the vine's roots —and continue slicing through the packed winter dirt and weeds. Then he repeated this on the next vine a few seconds later—as if in a sustained wrestling match. He and his team traveled slowly, no rush to finish, no accidents, comfortable moseying along and doing the work right.

Jackie and Molly knew the soil more than anyone else—perhaps even more than Dad, though in a different way. They understood the sandy loam areas that made for an easy pull following a spring shower and they knew the hardpan blocks where hidden rocks caught the plow and dragged it like an anchor. They felt the slightest incline or fall in the earth and made subtle adjustments. We benefited from their physical relationship with the land—a crucial connection for successful farmwork.

From the time when the horses and mules lived in the barn, a singletree and whippletree still hang against the wall, the pivoting, swinging bars to which the traces of the mules' harnesses were fastened. Missing are the full collar, the breast collar, and the harness, but still in evidence are the places where the animals leaned out the window and stall, rubbing against the wood, leaving their own marks, showing they lived and worked here, too. Dad never called what he did organic farming but it was: the farm was full of life, full of many lives that worked to grow more life that would then sustain others' lives.

"With the French plow and mules, work had a certain rhythm," Dad said. It was also hard, physical work.

I wish I had asked Dad how he worked with the mules. What did he say to get them going, did he really shout "whoa" to stop? I want to document the language of farming. I grew up driving a vineyard wagon while my folks sat on the wagon bed, dishing out scoops of fertilizer to tip under each tree. I grew familiar with their shouts and commands—*hooo* meant stop, *kay* to go forward. We were a people who knew how to communicate across a field and over the low rumble of a tractor engine.

The next innovation to the French plow added a retractable blade. As this cutting blade scraped against a vine trunk, it could be pushed out of the way by a strategically placed angle iron, then inserted back into place after safely passing the trunk. After the introduction of tractors, the driver (no longer the "wrestler" that my Dad had to be with his mule-drawn model) could control the blade, guiding it away from the vine. A kick arm was added, a type of trigger that helped sense when a vine stump was approaching. As the plow veered near the vine, the kick arm engaged a spring to help push and pull the plow in and out of a vineyard row.

French plowing can cause accidents and injuries that remain in the grapevines for a lifetime. I can see where I hooked a vine decades ago, though I reacted quick enough to clutch and brake and only moved the vine a foot. The roots held fast but stretched a bit, and from that point onward, the crooked vine stump became a reminder of that close call.

Sometimes, no matter how quick my reflexes, I have accidentally ripped out an entire vine from the earth. Ouch, that hurt. Whenever I drove past the vine gap (or worse, when Dad did), the empty spot memorialized the accident. I felt bad and still do. My father mourned. The vine died.

Nonetheless, I still French plow because it is usually beneficial to the plant. It slices away surface roots and encourages the vine to become deeply rooted, the most important characteristic of a grapevine. Some of our oldest vines at ninety years old have roots that go five to ten feet into the ground, searching out the minerals and nutrients that give them flavor. The plow also makes the soil healthy by turning it, mixing it with green grasses and weeds in order to build soil life and get it churning with all kinds of microbes.

Because I've been forced to live with my weeds, I am now learning more of them by name. Some escape the wrath of the French plow and are relatively harmless, like chickweed and purslane. In fact, many chefs devoted to organic, traditional cuisine use purslane, or pigweed, in salads and sauces. Edible landscaping uses it as a sustainable ground cover. Others, like Johnson weed, however, are evil and require deep plowing to dig out as much of the roots as possible. A few weeds that seem innocent in the spring, like mare's tail, trick me into ignoring them until it's too late and they poke out of the grape canopy, stealing sunlight, towering as high as ten feet.

Most important, saving this beneficial old practice and the indigenous knowledge of a farm and its farmers is valuable. Dad is relearning his own native competency and, in working with Dad, we are involved in an organic process that allows us to grow together. Memory and innate understanding of myriad connections count more than giving each other directions on how to French plow or shovel. Now I'm beginning to understand: Dad has no instructions to share but rather the wisdom of experience to be passed on.

French plowing links me with the past not in a nostalgic sense, but with a palpable connection to my father and our land. It has taught me the value of its particular kind of hard work and appreciation for what my father has accomplished. French plowing preserves a cultural tradition that spans my father's history from farm animals to machines, from working the fields with his parents as a child to working with his own children. Just as the plow is not just a piece of equipment, our farm is not just a mechanical framework for producing a commodity. The farm is an organic entity full of tradition, life, and change.

I smile every year when I finally finish French plowing. I think of improvements for next year yet recognize that the best and simplest solution is to—and I can still hear my father's voice whispering it—"Go slow."

Chapter Fourteen

HARDPAN ECONOMICS

A DENSE LAYER OF soil that usually hides just beneath the uppermost topsoil stratum—typically on our farm about two to four feet down—hardpan is largely impervious to water. Trees and plants larger than grasses can't grow on it because of the shallow root zone. Some hardpans were formed by deposits of clay in the soil that fused and bound together. Others are formed by compaction from repeated plowing or traffic.

Dad moved a mountain of hardpan, but hardpan has destroyed the spirit of many farmers.

Hardpan is the official rock of our farm. I don't believe I will ever free myself from its burdens.

A compressed layer of clay that behaves more like a rock than dirt, hardpan is a rather dull tan chunk of parched earth that looks like all life has been squeezed out of it. It lacks the nobility of granite or the texture of flagstone. Hiding a few feet beneath the surface, hardpan shocks unsuspecting farmers, gardeners, or builders who, trying to work the land, suddenly discover that shovels are worthless, pickaxes and sledgehammers more appropriate, and backhoes and dynamite the best.

Hardpan fields look like the surface of Mars, barren, red, arid, and empty—a landscape without spirit. (Imagine, sending a satellite or Rover mission 36 million miles into space only to discover hardpan.)

A layer of soil cemented by almost insoluble materials, hardpan is a rock that breaks farmers. The hardpan of the Central Valley was forming during the time of the dinosaurs, a hundred million years ago, when the land that would eventually become California was at the bottom of the Pacific Ocean. The collision of tectonic plates eventually pushed up a two-mile deep trench in that ocean floor to become the Central Valley. Our good loamy soil comes from the erosion of the mountains and volcanoes around us over millions of years after the valley's rise. Our hardpan dates back, though, to the hellish conditions of the land's first creation. Its violent birth was a preview to how, millions of years later, farmers would rage against it and bring their own explosive force to break it apart.

Dad was an expert on hardpan; he spent years clearing our fields of it. Our land was initially cheap because of its hardpan discount. No one had wanted it. Half of the land was filled with a fine Hanford sandy loam, where vigorous grapevines and sweet peaches and plums thrived. The other half was barren and open. Dad had made a choice: clearing this farm of hardpan would establish him. Otherwise he would have to keep renting, possibly one day saving enough to buy good land—if things worked out, if prices remained good, if the weather cooperated. Hardpan held the key to making a farm and building a family legacy. Dad didn't want to leave it up to fate; he wanted to work for himself.

He quickly named part of the farm "the hill," a slight rise on the horizon, perhaps only five to ten feet higher than the rest of the farm. But "the hill" hid a mountain of stone, a shallow layer of hardpan enclosing the virgin earth into which vines or an orchard could be planted and take root.

Dad spent two years clearing "the hill" of hardpan, in between farming the vineyard and orchard. A bulldozer came in to rip the soil open, and afterward a sea of rocks seemed to float in the earth like icebergs; tens of thousands of chunks. He dragged, carried, and heaved them onto wagons and truck beds, hauling tons away, claiming this land as his own. But after another pass of the bulldozer, the seemingly clear field would be blanketed once again with more stones. Progress was measured by the pairs of leather gloves he wore through and patched with black electrical tape wrapped around and over the holes in the fingertips.

At the end of the day, he'd come in, beat and exhausted, and lay those gloves on a workbench while he washed up for a late dinner. I could smell him in those extensions of his hands. His sweet sweat darkened the leather, the gloves stiff and rigid, holding the form of his hands wrapped around hardpan. As they lay there, they would slowly uncurl as if his fingers were opening painfully, having worked too long, locked in a death grip, unable to let go.

Hardpan comes in different sizes. Most pieces on the hill were small, only ten to twenty pounds; others were thousand-pound flat sheets of rock that had to be broken with pickaxe or sledgehammer. In some spots, even the bulldozer was unable to rip through the stone; the machine's claw bounced over underground piles that seemed determined to fight relocation. Dad had to use dynamite in order to break their grip, shattering the stronghold, allowing a tractor shank to hook the remaining chunks and loosen them from their antediluvian home. Back at the farmhouse, Mom herself was shaken with each blast, wondering who would get the best of the other: man or rock.

I don't believe Dad saw this massive earth removal as winning or losing. All he wanted was to get a foothold in the valley, not to conquer and control, but simply to make room to root a few vines and a family.

The hardpan of California's alien land laws and its culture from 1913 until the 1950s decreed that immigrants were to work the fields—not to own the fields. Exclusion acts often barred Asian women from immigrating, so some groups, such as the Chinese and

Filipinos, became bachelor societies, workers migrating to America as sojourners, unable to start families. Antimiscegenation laws barred interracial unions—in 1905 California declared illegal all marriages between whites and "Mongolians." Young nonwhite immigrant men were supposed to work hard, and when used up, they were supposed to go home.

Lack of financing kept some farmers trapped in a renting class. The typical rental agreements split the profits fifty-fifty between owner and renters. If he was lucky, the renter got a sixty-forty advantage, but that was rare. "When you rent, you're always working for someone else," Dad once told me. "And you'll never get ahead. In America, it's all about owning property."

Overcoming these social obstacles was no different than learning to live with hardpan. Once you clear a layer, you discover another layer, and a layer after that. Dad broke through and struggled with huge chunks, each in the way of roots and growth. Cultural barriers become walls of psychological discouragement. No single act prevents an individual from achieving success; inequality wounds and scars, bringing death and depression from a thousand cuts.

Dad worked with blinders of determination. He removed the mountain of hardpan one rock at a time. He started with the biggest rocks and accepted that there would always be small ones. Now a lush vineyard grows where that hardpan once choked our farm.

Occasionally a hardpan rock still surfaces, driven up by the freezing and thawing of the earth over the seasons. We whisper, "Damn," and pull it out, tossing it along the bank of the irrigation ditch that borders the former "hill." The bank has become a wall of stone protecting the vineyard from the swift currents of a nearby river, a further reminder of the work it has taken to stake a claim to this land.

Racial barriers can require generations to overcome. Old attitudes linger, as stubborn as hardpan. But the act of remembering acknowledges the past and helps break through misunderstanding and misconceptions to the truth of a deeper humanity and our common roots and desires. New immigrants continue to battle hardpan fields; families will always carry the burden of hardpan histories. Our family story was no different; history does repeat itself.

I saw this history in Dad's work gloves. Now I have my own work gloves and, like Dad, rarely throw them away. Many have holes torn in the right index finger or thumb from repetitive tasks, often wrapped with duct tape. A special pair was pigskin, which did not work well, since I'm too rough with my gloves and my work varies—one moment I'm driving tractor and a lightweight set of racing gloves could work well; next, I'll be jumping off the tractor to dig out and haul away a large chunk of hardpan. The weight of the heavy rock stretches and tears thin-skinned gloves.

My old gloves, like Dad's, hang around, some contorted into permanent fists, their final death grip. Like veterans, they seem to trade war stories as they crowd together in a workbench drawer, reminding me of their prior battles and our continuing struggles: they may be worn down but they have not forgotten.

Hardpan is tough, not very pretty, a symbol of survival for immigrant families who came to our valley to carve out a life for themselves. You don't work with hardpan if you're not planning on staying for a while. A metaphor for the valley, hardpan is a rock that doesn't like to be moved, like the conservative politics of this place, where traditions become embedded, adaptation is often slow, acceptance of differences difficult.

Just as hardpan was formed when pressurized silt and mud were cemented together by almost insoluble materials, so too do people often hunker down and harden when pressures from the outside challenge their ways of thinking. Some of my neighbors seem to be as stubborn as rocks, embedded in a place they don't want to leave but don't want to improve, blaming others for our problems. "Hardpan politics" thrive here; people have long memories, distrust outsiders.

Hardpan is indigenous to our lands and has kept a few areas wild and unfarmed. With today's decline in farms and poor crop prices, some of the first abandoned fields are those with uneven terrain and weak orchards and vineyards—signs of the presence of hardpan. These farms will revert back to their natural state, hardpan reclaiming her territory. I try to sustain the hardpan economics of hard work: I labor in a system where character matters, establish my own name and create a business that reclaims a past that acknowledges race and class history.

Even though I was privileged that Dad had removed much of our hardpan, when I returned to the farm, I quickly developed a relationship with this rock. Dad has passed down an addiction: I too lose myself in hardpan work, enjoying the satisfaction of extricating and exiling another rock, and then another. I marvel that Dad could have worked so damned hard for years and still keep a vision of a verdant, productive farm on that forbidding hardpan hill.

Yet I know that more hardpan lurks beneath the surface. I drag a disc and behind me a trail of hardpan bubbles up, floating in a sea of dirt. I try to ignore the rocks but they don't go away, reminding me of their presence with jolts and bumps on my next tractor pass, or after a rainstorm when, the loose dirt washed off, the cleansed rock surfaces shine and gleam in the sunlight. I can't ignore their taunts and envy neighbors who look relaxed, their fields unkempt, with areas of hardpan or Johnson grass or mounds that block irrigation water from ever reaching end vines or trees. Don't they notice the tree begging for water in the summer, leaves turning yellow and sometimes defoliating?

I am waiting for the rest of the nation to come back to our valley's best values, to return to the fiscally conservative nature of hardpan economics, where your actions speak the loudest, your works define who you are. Unfortunately, hardpan may have also created the foundation of a social and economic dichotomy. Hardpan communities embody the best and the worst of times and attitudes; local agricultural economies face a constant financial struggle with low-paying, seasonal employment.

Outsiders who do not understand the economic challenges of farming accuse all farmers of exploiting farmworkers. When they accused my dad, he answered, quiet yet powerful: at least these hardpan farms create jobs for people hungry for work. In his own way, Dad sought to help the few families who consistently worked for us. Paying the prevailing wages, he seemed a fair employer. I never heard him yell demands: he understood the hard labor that was required and remembered his own history in the fields. We often have the same workers return year after year, a good sign. Dad tried to treat people better than he had been treated, yet he understood the barriers that had caged his dreams and ambitions—hoping that each succeeding generation had the potential to be freer.

It will take time to improve our valley's poverty and social problems. We must measure progress with a timeline of seasons and generations. Dad set an example for me of self-reliance, clearing our fields of rocks one by one, load after load, trusting that, in the end, our family would find a way to survive and even thrive.

I once thought the best way to farm was to become a perfectionist, seeking to dispose of every rock and completely cleanse our fields. Now I allow myself to fail and accept the fact that I can't eliminate every piece of hardpan. It will always be part of us—the part that wants to purge the negative even when we know there will be more to follow. That's how Dad sees the cup, half full. (I once read a beer promotion on a coaster that read: "The pessimist sees the cup half empty; the optimist says: 'not for long'—and quickly gulps it down.")

Hardpan remains a dense rock; it will not take a hint and move away if I try to outwait it. I swear, it seems to procreate and give birth to families of stone. In fact, it does rise to the surface from below as the softer dirt compresses and (when wet) squeezes beneath a stone to push it upward, so that hardpan pops out on the surface like a newborn.

A symbol of Dad's fight to gain a foothold, hardpan measures our family's struggle to plant roots in America. It is a visible expression of Dad's effort to sow the seeds of values and of stories that continue to define me.

A curse of our valley that scars communities, hardpan makes

farm families bitter and hardened, forcing them to scratch out a living, to question their worth, and to wonder where they really belong.

Hardpan economics are the choices I made to take care of the land; opportunity costs—sacrifiing potential wealth by staying in the valley. In the end, I actually have no option but to choose Dad.

A slow lesson for me, hardpan may be invisible at times, hiding just beneath the surface. To survive, I have to find a way to live with it. Hardpan is not going away.

Chapter Fifteen

FALLING DOWN

A JAPANESE PARABLE: *"Nana korobi, ya-oki."* Fall down seven times, get up eight.

I never saw Dad fall down, even after his stroke. He usually managed to catch himself and regain his balance, his physical strength and enduring tenacity never letting him down completely—traits I admire. Yet by keeping your balance, you avoid the practice of falling then getting back up. Of course, as a business we often stumbled, and Dad usually responded by simply working harder. He never taught me how to fall down.

A few years following Dad's initial stroke, he had a series of smaller strokes. One knocked him off his feet and into a wheelchair for a while. He had to undergo more therapy, but something was different this time. He seemed to lack the will to try as hard.

Once, during therapy, we tried to teach him how to get up should he fall. He watched various methods. One was rolling on his side; another involved a step-by-step process of getting onto his knees. In order to practice, Dad first had to lie on the floor. But he refused. He refused to "fall" on the floor. Even if we held him and tried gently to drop him down into a prone position, he panicked. He would desperately reach and grab for his wheelchair. He would not allow himself to fall.

After he had returned home, he did stumble and fall in the yard. Mom tried to lift him, but he was too heavy. After a few minutes of struggle, he had exhausted himself and spent his energy. He lay prone, breathing deeply as Mom sought help from a neighbor. I arrived from the fields in time to see the neighbor help him to his feet and into a chair.

Drenched in sweat, Dad smiled, and waved to thank the neighbor. But I could tell he was not right. I believe he vowed never to fall again, that he denied what was inevitable, refusing to revisit the issue.

I have thought a lot about falling down, from physical to metaphoric failures. Perhaps we're allowed only so many major falls in our lifetime, a quota, and Dad had reached his limit. He no longer had the energy to get back up. I wonder how many falls I get. Of course, I fall better than Dad. I suppose this is not necessarily the ideal trait you want to surpass your father with, but it has merit.

As I've gotten older, I've learned the trick of how to fall without injuring myself. I wish this were something I could pass up to Dad. My father's inner strength may prove to be his greatest weakness. Whereas my ability—to fall with grace—may be my strength.

Let me tell you a story about a farm accident: I fell off my tractor. Actually, I was knocked off. By a tree limb. With a set of disc blades behind me.

My life did not pass before me—most farmwork moves much too slowly for that, and the speed of a typical tractor is slower than a walking pace. But this became a moment I will remember forever because it made me feel different about life: I had survived. And I had a story to pass on.

I was working in an old peach orchard with low-hanging limbs. Over the years, the trees had sagged lower and lower from the weight of many harvests; some branches had been poorly pruned and stuck out at awkward angles. We had strung rope around each tree, tightly wrapping the limbs, but often one or two limbs stubbornly protruded into the path of a tractor.

I was disking overgrown weeds, work that I should have done weeks earlier. But at that time, in May, I was racing to knock down some of the growth, impatient to get to other farm jobs that lay waiting.

Often old ropes break and dangle from the trees, so that I have to pull them out of the way as I drive. On this day, one hooked on the front of the tractor hood, so I first clutched with my left foot and then reached to snap the rope free. The tractor remained in gear because I intended to clutch for just a second or two. But the rope had tangled on something, so I had to stand in order to free it. I leaned forward and extended as far as I could.

Taking chances is part of the physical nature of farmwork. Most risks involve simple things, reaching out while tractoring to knock off a cluster of unwanted fruit, leaning on a shovel for balance as you vault over a muddy irrigation furrow, backing up in your truck, trying to see through a dust-coated rear window. I like to think of it as working on the edge.

In our information economy, the vast majority of people are removed from physical work and physical danger, insulated from the risks of working with their hands and bodies. On a farm, however, tightening finances demand that you work a little too fast, use older equipment, and try to take shortcuts, exposing yourself to nature's physical demands. It's all part of the gamble of farming.

I had overextended myself, misjudged my reach, and stretched too far. My left foot slipped off the clutch and the tractor leaped forward. Because I had been leaning on the steering wheel for leverage, a violent turn came with the jolt, a jerk to one side that suddenly flung me toward a low-hanging limb. Usually I can duck away from such obstacles, leaning to one side like a boxer dodging an incoming punch. Not this time. My face and chest were on a collision course with a fat branch. Someplace below me, the tractor continued to move forward.

I imagined being crushed between limb and tractor, my body bent and contorted. I could feel the tractor seat and tire fender squeezing me while the thick wood—more like a log—pushed me backward. Soon I would be trapped.

All this was unfolding in slow motion. Not because I was so acutely aware of impending danger but because tractors are geared to go very slowly. Fortunately, out of habit, I had throttled down when I had initially reached for the loose rope. So now the tractor cruised forward extra slowly while the immobile tree pressed into my chest. I had the choice of being crushed between limb and tractor or knocked backward off the tractor. The disc blades, all sixteen of them, awaited my falling body.

In a cartoon, a character would be flattened while goofy music played. Then the paper-thin character would get up with a ridiculous grin and pop back into normal shape. But this was not a cartoon. The danger was suddenly real. I felt helpless and dumb at the same time, either a preternatural calm before the pain and disaster or a sign of maturity that I could accept the factors over which I had no control in this situation.

I could not jump off the tractor, as the limb was already in my face. Luckily, my twenty-two-year-old peach trees have big limbs, sometimes a foot in diameter. Also, as trees age, much of the growth migrates to the top, where sunlight fosters the new wood, so my low-hanging limb did not have many small branches protruding that could pierce me, and it made a perfect climbing bar.

I reached and grabbed hold of the wood, wrapping my arms around the living log, clinging without thinking, my rear and legs still dangling. What better method to save myself than to trust my peach trees!

I was a converted tree hugger, a fifty-year-old farmer bonding with his orchard as his tractor slid away underneath him.

Yet my position was not normal or safe. I had slipped off the seat as the tractor moved away from me and now was riding atop the large rear tires. First my butt then my legs bounced on the ridges. I had never had this sensation before, as you're not supposed to ride on top of a rolling tire. As the tire churned beneath me, I could feel the watch in my hip pocket getting crushed over and over with each deep grove in the tractor tire. I could tell that my hip and thigh bones were likewise being battered—a most peculiar sensation, to feel something you never felt before and never imagined and never want to repeat.

But the tree limb held, as did my own lower limbs. I bounced, the tractor eased forward on its own and for a moment I thought: *It's working!* My legs seemed to be intact, and I thought that I could simply then swing down to the ground. But then the disc blades came into view.

This was not good. So I pulled myself up and lifted my lower body. Glancing down I could see the yellow tandem and shiny blades glide below. They passed slowly, turning the weeds and slicing them into the earth, a nice clean farm chore, seen from a rare point of view.

The tractor and disc slid below me without incident and I could safely come out of the tree. I dropped to the ground, landed gently in the turned earth, and stood erect like a prizewinning gymnast sticking my landing. Fortunately, all things pass.

Someone or something was watching over me. I felt grateful; I had been granted a do-over, one of the few times in life when something right happened. I felt as if I now I had to make a life list—things I want to do before it is too late, a list of good deeds and good acts. Was it a moral obligation because I had been granted a reprieve? I felt a newfound intention to live in the present, recognize the fragility of life, and make a difference in the world moment by moment.

I had been saved by the peach limb, the very limb that originally knocked me off the tractor. Was this a glimpse into the interconnected world of nature?

Or perhaps I had simply learned something about humility and the everyday world of those who engage in physical labor. The risks we take are democratic; we have equal opportunity to be injured. Yet in many professions like farming, the inherent dangers remain invisible: we lack the public recognition that practitioners of an extreme sport receive. Everyone eats dangerous food, not because there's a health risk to the consumer but because the farmer and farmworker are endangered as they cultivate it. And farming systems won't become easier—it's part of working with nature—someplace in the food chain someone is always going to be doing backbreaking, physically draining work. Someone has to.

So for a few seconds, I basked in the warmth of having survived something. As the tractor drove slowly away, I felt complete. I stood admiring the situation: a major accident had been avoided, my stupid act of leaning to pull a rope out of the way had not resulted in a major injury. I patted my body. My chest, hips, and legs were still intact; I had no bleeding, no internal damage or broken limbs. I had escaped whole. I was happy.

Until I realized that the tractor was working its way down the row, amazingly still going straight. I thought: *So this is what it looks like for a tractor to be driverless?*

Then I gasped. *Wait, I'm the driver of that driverless tractor.*

Rational thoughts returned to my mind. I could no longer be the observer. This is real and I had to be responsible. *Run. Catch that tractor.*

So I dashed to overtake the machine, which required only seconds. The familiar step I had climbed thousands of times before looked a little different in motion, but in one quick jump I was on and seated.

By now, the front wheels had turned and were heading directly for a tree. I jammed down the clutch and rolled to a stop. All was still.

I sat quiet for a moment, then turned off the tractor. It rumbled to a stop and we both paused. I caught my breath. I thought about what just had unfolded. It had been like a dream, but it was real. Real lucky. Stupid. Fortunate. I looked back and saw the low limb that had become my friend forever. Unreal.

I planned to tell Dad the story, to share the details of the fall, the thoughts that raced through my mind, the danger, the rush, the luck. I imagined he would smile gently, nod his head, and listen. He wouldn't nod out of approval; no one plans on falling down. He would nod from experience, comparing my adventure to his. We share in the story. We get back up to tell the story.

I will go home to share this all with Marcy. When she asks why I've come in from work early, I will shake my head in disbelief. It still doesn't seem real.

I will begin: "Let me tell you a story. . . ."

Part Four

Planting Memories

Chapter Sixteen

WELDING

The day Dad had his stroke, I had come back to the shed because I had broken the French plow and hoped to find Dad so he could fix it. I had been driving too fast and hooked a deep vine root and stake. For a moment, machine and nature were locked in battle. Something snapped, and the tractor and plow shook as they broke free. I could hear the metal bending and hit the clutch. A dust cloud exploded and, as I waited for it to settle, I could see that the machine was contorted. When I slowly raised the tractor hydraulics, the plow hung limp—bent, damaged, and injured.

Dad had been a repair man for his entire life. He fixed things. Uncles and neighbors would drop by to ask Dad to fix something for them and he'd stop to help them, even though it took him away from his own work and plans. He had difficulty saying no, but he also seemed content helping others, and his favor was followed by an extended visit and conversation. I was no different from others—when things broke, I depended on Dad.

When Dad worked with metal, he cut it with an oxyacetylene torch and then employed an old Lincoln arc welder to fuse pieces together. He showed me how to cut and weld, but since he was so good, I could never achieve his skill level, so I didn't pay enough attention, selfishly assuming that Dad would always be around to fix things.

I like the drama of welding, beginning with the costume. Dad would put on a heavier old work shirt, protecting himself and his clothes from the flying sparks. Then he pulled on thick heavy leather gloves with protective sleeves that came halfway up his arms. Finally, for the oxyacetylene cutting, he wore a backward Giants baseball cap and donned black-shaded goggles; tiny specks of hardened metal from years of cutting spotted the lenses. For arc welding, he put on an ancient welding helmet, a black mask that covered and protected the entire face and neck area from the heat and sparks. It had only a narrow blackened-glass eye slit to see through. If I were helping, I'd put on the same garb. As kids, my siblings and I had sometimes played with the helmet, pretending to be robots from a 1950s movie like *The Day the Earth Stood Still*. Wearing that dark helmet, we ordinary farm kids felt as if we were transported into the future.

To use the oxyacetylene torch, Dad began by opening valves on two tanks, one filled with oxygen and the other acetylene. The gas passed through hoses to combine in a brass torch. When ignited by a spark from a striker, the gases produced an extremely high-temperature flame. The steady hiss of the gas filled the air. The smell of heated metal, a sharp aroma, dirty and, if I could attach a color, the scent of brown. A feather of black smoke rose as Dad leaned over the object of our triage, a bright orange light at the point of contact.

Dad heated the metal until it was cherry red; depending on the thickness, this required from a few seconds to a half minute. Then, in a reaction that amazed me every time I saw it, the solid metal transformed into a liquid. Exactly at the point of contact, a tiny puddle of molten steel danced beneath the flame. The seemingly invincible steel had changed. A world of possibilities had opened.

To increase the heat, Dad squeezed a trigger on the torch that added a controlled stream of oxygen, which blew through the steel. The cut began. The hiss became a sizzling sound as the metal burned. Moving slowly along a line he had drawn with chalk, Dad cut the steel, sparks flying and slag dripping. Afterward, the metal edge revealed a band of vertical lines, a sign of a clean, even cut. Dad's signature.

Dad also welded like an artist. He had bought his used Lincoln arc welder decades before. Its red paint had faded and the ancient tool resembled an old upright radio from the Great Depression, the type families once gathered around in the living room. On the front was a handle that controlled the amount of voltage and a simple switch that turned on and off with a sharp click. As soon as it clicked on, the current sang through the transformer and set up a hum of energy.

Electricity carries a palpable feel of excitement. With arc welding, the goal is similar to oxyacetylene work: burn metal, transforming the solid into a liquid. An electric current passes through cables to a clamp the welder holds that itself holds a welding rod or stick, which gets heated to the melting point so that it streams into the welding seam. This becomes the positive electrode. A negative clamp is attached to the metal object that you want to weld. When the stick is held close to the metal, leaving a tiny gap, the electricity arcs and the extremely hot current melts the rod. If done properly, the molten metal bonds deep within the surfaces, fusing two separate entities into one.

The trick of course is proper spacing of the rod and metal. Too far and there's no arc, too close and the rod or stick will fuse itself to the metal, short-circuiting the system. When the arc melts the rod or stick to form a puddle, the technique is to push or pull the puddle across the metal joint so that it penetrates the surface, sometimes making a slight circular motion, creating tiny waves of metal in the puddle. Dad understood how to build a welded joint so that it was strong and deep, both edges fused together. When his best welds hardened and cooled, they looked like tiny ribs of steel bonding two pieces. His seams were pure artistry.

Dad's skill also manifested itself in his ability to see through the tinted eye lens of the helmet, which was so dark that it always defeated me. The eye window is a narrow horizontal rectangle of tinted glass that protects eyes from the arc's dangerously high ultraviolet and infrared waves. This flame can burn a blue impression into the cornea and inflame the tissue, like staring at the sun. Even when looking through the glass in full sunlight, however, I could not see my hands in front of me. But Dad would position the metal and the rod close together, flip down the helmet (sometimes with a quick nod of the head), and then, in almost total blackness, move the electrode close enough to spark the arc. Once started, the intense light of the arc illuminated his work.

Dad had developed his skill from trusting his memory and from practice. I tried many times but could not master his technique. Sightless, I'd jab at the metal with the rod so that sparks would fly. My heart would race and I'd quickly pull back and lose the arc. I'd hold the stick too close and it would fuse with the metal in a fraction of a second so that I'd have to shake it in order to break it loose. Sometimes I would have to whip the electrode holder violently, snapping it free from the target metal and in the process knocking over the piece I was trying to weld. I simply could not get started.

A few months following Dad's stroke, I try to modify a disc by removing four center blades to create a gap so that the strip of lush cover crops down each row in the vineyards and orchards would escape disking and thrive. In order for the remaining twelve blades to fit tightly, however, I have to make a spacer blade by cutting a regular blade down to its core, reducing it from twenty inches in diameter to about six. I set up for what should be a simple operation and roll out the oxyacetylene torch. Dad joins to watch.

Since this modification does not require a very precise cut, this might be a good test for Dad. I help him put on gloves and protective eye goggles, then ignite the torch and pass it on to him.

The few seizures Dad had since his initial stroke have left his hands unsteady. Even though he starts successfully to make a cut, it's difficult for him to keep the torch flame in one place. The torch makes a popping noise, a sign he's too close to the surface. Twice he suffocates the flame by hitting the nozzle against the metal, momentarily stopping the gas and losing the ignition. We stop. I relight the torch.

Because he moves unevenly, Dad can't control the heat in order to let it intensify enough to make a puddle of the metal. The edges of the cut are jagged, too hot in some places, not hot enough in others. Because he can't control his hands, he begins to distrust them. I suggest we wait a few more months and try again. We both nod, knowing that won't happen. Dad will never weld again. But because he can't speak, I can't tell if he accepts this failure—is he satisfied to live without this skill in which he took such pride and for which he was so admired? Or is it easy to set it aside, given the other challenges that occupy him every day?

For the next few months I work in fear. What will I do if something breaks? Because I am a poor welder I devise strategies: First, I try to be more careful and avoid accidents. This may work for a while, but accidents are precisely that, accidents that I cannot foresee or forestall. Second, I won't attempt to fix minor problems but learn to live with them. This works, but I'm just delaying payment—small problems don't go away, they return as bigger ones. Third, I try to convince myself to throw away broken things and buy new, which is feasible only in between necessary repairs. Otherwise it would quickly become too expensive. I regret not learning more from Dad. I was the breaker, he was the fixer. I was fast, Dad was slow. A symmetry between father and son.

I can never be a fixer like Dad, but I can try again to improve my welding. Declaring my student status frees me to learn. Since I can't see the way Dad sees, I buy a new arc welding helmet, which has a modern lens-shade system—transparent material that darkens automatically when exposed to the flare of the welding arc. I don't have to spend years apprenticing and practicing or try to develop the body memory and feel that was part of Dad's skill. I don't trust myself to weld blindly, and with the new helmet, I don't have to. My welding improves. I can control the rod and arc much better, creating a more even flow and consistent seam. My welding has rhythm, my best seam looks like tiny fish scales layered upon one another, stacked in a row. With new energy and confidence, I tackle some minor repairs that have been looming.

One in particular is fixing our disc. Over the years, the frame has bent slightly from tilling the earth and turning weeds in the orchard rows. This defect places extra strain on an angle iron near the hydraulic ram, which lifts the frame off the ground for turning and transport. Soon that bend in the frame will snap, bogging me down in an avenue with its collapse, and requiring a much more costly repair. I've welded it in place, reinforcing it with another piece of iron, but it won't hold for long. If I can reweld it and add another metal plate for support, that should prevent an untimely breakdown.

Confidence changes everything. Before I attempt to rework the weakened joint, I decide to remove the angle iron that I had sloppily attached, knowing I can now easily reattach it with a better weld (thanks to my helmet). Once clear of the patchwork of repairs, the frame looks different and I can see that the frame actually needs only a single, very strong weld in a crucial pressure point. Part of the fix will require a vertical upward weld, not so easy to do. I can do vertical welds going downward, but that would be a weaker solution. Imagine two pieces of metal sitting upright. In order to be fused together, the corner joint where the two sides meet must be securely welded. If I were to start at the top, gravity would pull the puddle of molten metal down and I'll race and go too fast. The weld won't penetrate the metal, but run, drip, and pool. Moving up with a weld piles drops onto cooling drops, little building blocks. The crucial question I should have asked Dad before it was too late: "How do you push a puddle upward?" It sounds like a Zen koan, but he could have shown me.

Dad's expert welding may also have stemmed from his ability to visualize and design, much like an engineer. When something broke, he started to repair it by first studying how it had been put together. Sometimes he even improved on the original by adapting it to our particular farming operation and needs. With his great sense of how to frame problems, welds were the final, not the first step. Prior to reattaching another repair plate to the disc, I emulate Dad and reconsider the design of the disc frame. I suddenly see that fastening an angle iron with bolts should provide just as much strength. And it will require only some spot welds.

A weld is just part of a whole, but it can of course be strong and integrated into the form and structure of a tool or be a weak Band-Aid masquerading as a repair. The design of a machine keeps all the pieces in place with minimal connections, but there is a central, organic frame at the heart of every structure that gives it the power and strength to perform the task for which it was created.

So, too, is there a central frame to a fruit tree. Its six to eight main branches create the integral form and function of the tree's vitality and ability to bear fruit. As stewards of our trees, we have to "repair" bends in their limbs—we prop up some branches with wooden props, or we wrap them with ropes so they don't bend too far and break. Arborists working on old ornamental trees will cable the thick old limb of oaks and maples to their main trunks so they don't snap under pressure from wind, rain, or ice. That's what the angle iron would do for our disc when I welded and bolted it. The disc's design will provide the organic frame for my machine—shore it up and strengthen it to lengthen its useful life, as well as its utilitarian beauty.

When Dad wanders into the shed after his day of shoveling weeds, I show him my redesigned fix of the wheel disc using the spot welding and thick bolts. He nods, which reassures me, even though I'm not sure he completely understands. Even so, I'm excited and can now work without fear on the repairs. I am also freed from my fear of breakdowns and accidents in the fields. After my next accident, I'll immediately start redesigning the repair project as I'm driving back to the shed, before I start cutting and rewelding.

Welding is a solitary act, man on machine, one on one, pushing puddles of molten metal across a surface. I get lost in the transformation of the metal, mesmerized by the flame turning matter into fluid, by my shepherding of its flow into the right lines and spaces using a steady and smooth rhythm, and by the weld turning from a repair into an integral part of the machine. As I make my final welds, I look up and see Dad helping to clean up, gathering wrenches I had scattered, rolling up the oxyacetylene hose, and waiting for me to finish.

It's now late in the day. Enveloped by the repair job, I had lost track of time, lost in work. With the oxyacetylene torch, I cut a final small piece of angle iron that will be set in place with welding. I'm standing next to a faucet, running cool water over the cherry hot metal before attaching it.

I turn to Dad and thank him for cleaning up after me. "You used to spend hours back here, cutting and welding, fixing . . ." I say. "Do you miss it?"

Dad shrugs. His face droops, an upside-down smile, not a smirk or display of anger, but a sad clown face. He shrugs and tilts his head from side to side.

"Yeah, I know," I answer.

The steel hisses under the stream of cooling water.

Chapter Seventeen

KILLING AN ORCHARD TO SAVE THE FARM

WE'RE TAUGHT NOT to judge other people by the color of their skin. Our taxonomy of good and bad is not supposed to be based on superficial indicators. Yet color is used to differentiate superior and inferior in the foods we eat, and it is not always the best natural indicator of ripeness or quality. The uniform, stereotypically primary colors of mass-produced fruits and vegetables fool our eyes. Heirloom varieties with their different appearances often have superior qualities, their beauty deeper than their skins.

The truck's brakes groaned as it came to a stop in a cloud of dust next to our old orchard of nectarines in 1978. The trailer could barely contain the bulldozer, and part of the Caterpillar's tracks bulged over the sides. But soon the yellow beast crawled down off the trailer and turned into the fields, its diesel engine churning. The driver wore shaded goggles and an air filter mask. I could not see his face as he swung the monster into place, lining up in front of the first row. Then he gunned the engine, the motor roared in response, and, with a blast of black smoke, it began to kill the orchard.

The first tree resisted. But the dozer's front fork slipped underneath the tree's roots, snapping decades of growth and toppling the plant, a cloud of dust exploding into the air. The crack of the first limbs shot over the countryside and I imagined other farmers and farmworkers looking up from their labor, trying to determine the origins of the sharp destructive snap, never a good sound in an orchard.

Within an hour, the first row was pushed over, a column of fallen giants. The yellow machine had executed its role perfectly, leaving nothing alive behind it. An apocalyptic scene, it was as if a great civilization lay in ruins.

Dad and I watched quietly as the bulldozer methodically continued its work. Then Dad turned and left.

During the summer of 1978, yellow-skinned peaches and nectarines were unappealing and unsalable. That's what we were told by our brokers and, judging by our lack of monetary returns, that statement was valid.

In the 1970s, as corporate farming and distribution took hold, a homogenization of food crops also occurred. New uniform-looking red hybrids supplanted a diversity of older varieties of peaches and nectarines. Some of the old varieties had once been revolutionary themselves. From the 1950s to 1978, for instance, Dad grew a wonderful nectarine called Le Grand. Developed in the 1940s by Fred Anderson from Le Grand, California, it was one of the first large nectarines and could be transported without as much damage as others suffered, which meant that they looked good on arrival at markets. Its yellow-red color was beautiful, particularly compared with older varieties that had green skins when ripe and bruised easily. But just as the blush nectarines had supplanted green ones, the reds supplanted the Le Grands—although in this case, Le Grands tasted better than the harder, brighter, newer fruit. Nonetheless, we couldn't move our heirlooms.

Because I had only just returned to the farm after college in 1976, I hadn't been paying much attention to prices until then. I naively had assumed that people and produce were paid what they were worth, according to the basics of supply and demand. Work hard; make good money. Good taste was rewarded with good prices.

Dad had asked me to handle the harvests, which was a huge step in my education as a farmer. I thought it was because he thought I was better at handling our labor, as Dad's quiet, reserved nature was not always best suited to dealing with people. But I see now that it was because he could tell that farming was undergoing bigger changes and he wanted me to experience them firsthand, so that I could learn how to deal with them. Increasing regulations required farmers to spend more time inside at a desk reporting and documenting their business instead of out in the fields, for instance. But besides the growth in government interference, Dad sensed another shift in the business of farming. It was subtle at first, but by 1978 flavor had been usurped by color and appearance. This new business language of growing fruit with its changes in standards and its reduction in the valuation of his work confused Dad.

At that time, supermarkets and large grocery stores had begun to dominate the marketplace. Large amounts of stone fruit—peaches, plums, and nectarines—were in demand, and the new varieties produced bigger fruit in larger volumes in the public's favorite color—red. Brokers were demanding (and rewarding) red fruit. We farmers were being enslaved by color, and consumers' choices were being dictated by color.

After years of getting poor prices, even I had to admit that when I held an older, yellow heirloom next to a shiny new red one, my eyes, too, gravitated toward the red. My perception had been retrained. Red had become the symbol of acceptance and success. Redder masqueraded as better.

Perhaps some of this change in preference stemmed from the spread of color televisions in America in the 1960s. Like Dorothy awakening in the cinematic, full-color Land of Oz after black-and-white Kansas, color exploded into our sensibilities, influencing our preferences. Big red peaches and nectarines seemed to carry the promise of something good, whereas our paler, less assertive yellow fruit with its delicate red blush seemed somehow less desirable. Consumers began to trust their eyes and abandon their past experiences of flavor. Others who'd never had nectarines before the bigger, tougher, more transportable red ones appeared simply assumed that's the way all nectarines looked and tasted. As the fruit industry grew larger, a longer shelf life also became more important. The full-bodied, complex tastes of the past were erased, replaced by a monochromatic plastic look and flavor. Memory and a sense of history were excluded from consumer transactions, thrown away—along with the older heirloom varieties . . . and old farmers.

Industry leaders argued that farmers and distributors needed to work together to maintain and increase quality and establish California fruits as superior to fruit from other states. They sought to assure retailers that our marketing regs guaranteed that every piece of fruit would meet specific standards. For the farmer, the new buyers of large volumes of fruits were not individual consumers but the larger grocery store chains, with their demands for uniformity.

The dominance of bright red colors in the tree fruit industry was ensured with the introduction of the color chip. Since 1933 all peach and nectarine growers in California had worked under marketing regulations that had the power to set quality standards. In order to help regulate supply in the late 1970s, researchers demonstrated a relationship between the color of fruit and its maturity or ripeness. Afterward, dozens of different varieties were categorized and assigned a color chip as a standard by which that fruit would be harvested. Color chips were a series of small cards, each printed with a distinct shade, ranging from green to yellow. A small hole, about an inch in diameter, was cut in the middle of each chip. Using the assigned color chip for each variety, USDA inspectors who visited farms during harvests examined fruit as it was packed into boxes, searching for the greenest part and placing the card over that spot. If that spot appeared greener than the chip hue assigned that variety, it was classified as not mature and its harvest would be stopped.

Because of this standardization of color—not of flavor or nutrition content—newer varieties that got redder earlier were introduced annually. As the system rewarded redder colors, farmers and nurseries played along by planting varieties that had more color.

Using color as the sole indicator of quality is wrong. It smacks of the nonsensical overregulations in Orwell's *Animal Farm:* all animals are equal, but some animals are more equal than others. Redder nectarines, no matter how they tasted, were considered better than our yellow ones. Cosmetic standards devalued content and meaning.

Dad saw that our Le Grands would struggle to make the grade in the face of new regs and constant evaluations. And they simply were not selling. Dad was fifty-six years old in 1978, I was twenty-four; yet we both were being driven out of business by the tyranny of the majority.

The answer was to retool our farm. Plant new varieties. Dad hesitated, because he hated to be part of this oppressive system, and he knew that our other heirloom varieties, such as the Sun Crest peaches, would soon face a similar trial and prosecution. Yellow had been defined as unmarketable. It was unwanted. This must have hit Dad as an insult. He was often judged by the color of his skin—and now, as frivolous as it sounded, so were his fruits.

The death blow came with Fantasia, a new, shiny, and very red nectarine variety that was developed by the USDA in the mid-1970s and broadly released. Thousands of acres of Fantasia were planted, and the fruit appealed to consumers like eye candy—it was a visual thrill to buy. Our delicious, pale Le Grands could not compete.

Our eighty-acre farm, which had seemed to be about the right size for Dad and me, suddenly felt wrong. Did we need to expand, make more room for new varieties, or downsize and destroy those orchards that required more management and plant raisin grapes instead? Grapes don't require as much attention, they are a more forgiving crop—and no one judges raisins by their color. I even thought about getting a city job and getting off the farm. Dad did not want me to be enslaved to a dying operation.

Trapped by the majority's expectations for nectarines, we decided that euthanasia of our old, off-color Le Grand nectarines was the humane option for both the farm and the farmers. So Dad called in the bulldozer to kill our three hundred beautiful, healthy, productive heirloom trees.

After they'd been uprooted, we burned the dead trees. The leaves had dried and were easily ignited; the trunks and dangling limbs looked like corpses, inviting cremation. We watched in silence. Whereas once these trees had covered us in their flowery scents of spring and the honeyed smells of nectar at harvest, now our clothes smelled of smoke and our eyes burned from the dry fumes. When Dad turned to go, I asked, "Do I need to stay until the end?" He didn't answer.

Even though he cannot talk now, Dad and I revisit memories. I find an old box we once used to pick and haul in peaches and nectarines from the field and that had MASUMOTO printed on the side. Dad grins when he sees it again, like meeting an old friend. We think of all the old fruit varieties that the box once held, fruits to which we were proud to attach our name.

Can Dad make new memories? We talk about planting another variety, perhaps something that ripens at the end of the season. We already have twenty acres of peaches, perhaps another nectarine will work well with our variety mix. But it has to fit into our other fruits' schedules. I've learned that I can manage the farm as long as work develops in stages, especially with stone-fruit harvests. We can't pick them all at once and need to stagger the starting harvest dates of each variety.

I check in with Mom, who for decades kept track of each day we picked fruit, the variety and start date. She consults her notebooks and the next day hands over a small pocket-sized notebook with records from 1966 to 1979, which shows that after we finished the Sun Crest Peaches, we always started the Le Grand within a few days.

Le Grand. The name brings a smile to both Dad's and my faces. I want to replant Le Grand nectarines as a living memorial to Dad. Besides, it fits our seasons and could be a wonderful way to complete our annual tree fruit harvest. We recover part of our past with memories of this fruit. Yellow is good, especially in the new organic markets. Our buyers these days search out great flavor and remember it, and our fruits reclaim memories—of nature's diversity, of culture and heritage.

Farming is a cultural act. Poet-activist Wendell Berry writes of "eating as an agricultural act" and describes an ideal world where consumers are not passive but play an active role in farming. They vote with their dollars and their consumption patterns. I believe in this power, but I also believe that agriculture itself must be personal. Food should embody a sense of history and manifest the terroir—the taste of the place where it grows, its elemental nature. It should also embody the human element that nurtures it and gives it life through our farmwork. All who eat participate in the culture of farming.

Farming is unpredictable, not controlled or controllable. It's about surviving, but not about survival of the fittest. It is imbued with memories of the past. Culture, not just economics, has a place at our table.

I locate a single Le Grand tree in another old farmer's backyard and will prune scion wood for winter grafting. I tell Dad of my plan. Dad listens and nods. I believe he understands.

The next day I find an old hand stamp placed next to my work gloves in my pickup. Dad has located the old Le Grand stamp we once used decades ago on our fruit boxes. Originally the rubber stamp was longer and wider, spelling out *Late Le Grand*, a variety we had also grown that was harvested a few weeks after Le Grand.

After Dad had pulled out the aging Late Le Grand orchard years ago and replaced it with Le Grand (and being a savvy businessman), rather than purchasing a new stamp, Dad simply took a sharp knife and cut off the "Late" part of the name. No longer "late," they'll now be reborn on our farm. Dad has passed the old stamp on to me. With it, I can reuse and renew his memory.

Chapter Eighteen

THE SWEAT THESIS

WORK AS A craftsman, sweat as an artisan. The art of farming keeps you going.

Dad taught me how to sweat by sweating.

On the farm, we don't wear deodorant. We don't cover up sweat stains on our clothing. Trees and vines don't judge us if we look sweaty and stressed. They don't associate sweat with dirt, perspiration with ineptitude. They don't worry about appearances.

Dad once told me, "Don't farm if you don't like sweat." No good farmer avoids sweating. We like the aroma of human work.

Not many people understand sweat. Sweat defines the character of our farm and the valley we call home. In the summer, air gets trapped between the Sierra mountains and the Coast Ranges. With nowhere to go, the heat pushes downward, compressing the air, generating more heat, creating an inversion, a natural solar oven. (Inversions in our valley combine with air pollution from vehicle exhaust and industries, trapping smog; we have "bad air days," proclaimed by local health officials as cases of asthma and lung problems explode.) Peaches and nectarines love the heat. Only because we're committed to our farms do we also tolerate these conditions. Love conquers all.

When I sweat, it appears first on my chest, seeping through my pores, subtle and silent, onto bare skin. A damp chill tickles and tricks me for a moment, then my body sends a simple message—"hot." My clothes cling to my body and I grow conscious of my heavy breathing. I can feel moisture in my hair. It beads on my forehead, drips down my temples, and slips across my cheeks. It beads on my upper lip, where I can taste its salty tang. It seeps into my eyes, where it burns and blinds. I blink and it stings more, forces me to work slow or stop, waiting for tears to wash my eyes clean. I wipe away the perspiration with my shirtsleeve and shake my head to keep it out of my eyes. Sweat reminds me of limits. I'm losing liquids. I can't go forever, have to stop sometime.

When I sweat, T-shirt and work shirt get soaked first, followed by hat and gloves, underwear and socks. A few scorching days have been so hot that even my leather belt is stained. The only parts of my clothes never soaked with sweat are my pants belt loops.

Dad, too, sweats, but he paces himself and knows his limits. After his stroke, I watch his sweat for warning signs. The faded blue work shirt gives away his body temperatures—first, his back gets wet spots, then his armpits darken, acting as a heart monitor and thermometer. Dark stains warn that it's time for intervention and I join him to help with his weeding, or I give him water so that we both can take a break from our work. Dad has learned to live with sweat. He understands what his body is telling him.

We euphemistically call our summer weather "dry heat," when temperatures rocket to 110 degrees once or twice a summer, usually with very little humidity. A method called "dry heat sterilization" is used in cleaning medical instruments, and I sometimes think of that when I'm working in 115 degrees, hoping it's keeping me healthy. Dry heat is also part of the heat index, comparing humidity levels and temperature to determine how hot it feels. Before his stroke, I once tried to explain this definition of heat index to Dad, exploring the intricacies of "the human-perceived equivalent temperature range" and the difference between our heat and the heat in other parts of the country. Dad politely listened and asked, "When it's one hundred and ten degrees, do you really care?" I stopped my research.

I think of our sweat as clean and honest. The South's high, sticky humidity levels gradually suck energy out of me. I grow weary sweating in muggy weather. The cooler summers of the Midwest send a chill across my damp chest and confuse my senses. When I sweat, I like to feel hot. Our valley heat quickly drains me, but, with enough liquids, I can be replenished. Oddly, I sometimes feel cleaner when I sweat, my pores opening, unlike the sweat I get in big cities, where the feel of grime penetrates my lungs and coats my skin. There I rub my arm with my fingers and create a smudge, a blend of smog, soot, and perspiration.

I identify with those in construction or on road crews who sweat hard. Hot, hot days bond us laborers. We want to start with the first sunlight, daybreak at 5:30 a.m., to beat the heat and delay the sweat a little. We sweat laborers wear universal badges of honor, work shirts darkened with moisture and later deposits of white sodium, blotches on our clothes and across our chests. The sweat stains on the brim of our hats mark us as veteran field hands and tell the world we work "out there," in the blast furnace of the real world. Sweat and work will burn in our memories.

The ungodly heat can kill. Heat exhaustion can trick you, because your skin can stay cool and moist even as other symptoms arrive that we often assume are only part of work: muscle cramps, headaches, and weakness. But when we feel dizzy and nauseated, we take our sweat seriously, because heatstroke may be imminent, with its confusion and disorientation, precursors to a heart attack.

Sweat is involuntary, heat the usual source. But in an air-conditioned car, I've felt warm moisture break across my skin—generated by stress and nerves—like driving fairly fast and suddenly seeing a police car or state trooper in my rearview mirror. Then, as the cop cruises by . . . my heart slows, I relax, and the moisture stops. I think of this as perspiration, not sweat. You can't stop sweating that easily. Similarly, the sweat from exercising at the gym is self-inflicted and can be stopped at any time. Bottom line—it's not work.

By sweating, the body releases fluids to cool you down. Horses sweat and need to be wiped and brushed. Dogs can't sweat; they pant and hang their tongues out and perspire through the pads of their paws. The expression "sweat like a pig" is incorrect, because the swine family doesn't have the glands to sweat and have difficulty dissipating heat. That's why they lie in the mud, wallowing in something cool to keep their body temperatures low.

I consider myself a master of sweat. I have even studied how to live with it. I used to stay in the same work clothes throughout the day—after all, why change, I'll just sweat more in the afternoon and evening. But I found that I could renew my energy by changing my T-shirts often. During our valley's annual run of 105-degree consecutive days, I'll change my shirts three to four times, draping them over the farmhouse porch rail to dry stiff in the sun. When Marcy returns from her job as an education project director and drives into our yard at the end of the day, she can count the shirts to determine how hard a day I've had. Changing shirts tricks me into thinking I'm refreshed and can go right back out, but it's also a method of pacing myself and making myself take a few breaks, even as I accept the fact that there's more work to do that will create more sweat.

Weather reports could forecast a sweat index using my T-shirt count. A hot day is a one- or two-shirt day, very hot may be a three-shirt day, and a killer heat wave demands four or more. I ran out of shirts on the worst day this past summer and was forced to recycle one from the morning. It felt dry, but the aroma kept it from being as refreshing as a clean one.

Sweat and work transform us and make our livelihood different. Not many people will stoop to laboring in such extreme conditions and sacrifice themselves.

"It comes with the territory," Dad would say, meaning it both figuratively and literally.

Dad and I bond with sweat, sharing in a daily ritual and rite of passage, in the same weather, temperature, and climate. We work under the same sun. We often lie about the sweat, convincing ourselves it could be worse as we trudge back outside for more abuse.

The best liars are farmers. Harvesttime comes with heat (that's how plants usually work), and we have no choice but to work in it—fields need to be watered, weeds shoveled, peaches and grapes picked. Ask farmers: "Can you work in spite of the heat?" They answer with a slight nod, perhaps an impish grin—and know they lie when they say, "No sweat."

Sweat and heat sometimes reduce Dad and me to nothing. We can get lost in the heat wave, dwarfed by the pressure of the temperatures and the burden of caring for thousands of trees and vines. Suddenly we feel small, our work insignificant.

During a twenty-day heat wave with temperatures between 105 and 115 degrees, we become invisible. The summer sunrise begins with temperatures in the 70s; by noon it's 100. Work continues in 110-degree heat, a hellishly ubiquitous heat like a furnace with no escape exit door. Hot. We're foolish to be out in this kind of heat, but Dad and I both know: grapes and peaches cry for water. If we're thirsty, so are they.

The work and heat beat us. We pant like dogs. Take short breaths, saving energy, feel our hearts race and veins and arteries pulsate. We lean over, hands on knees, sweat dripping from our faces. I want to quit; it's not worth it, I think. Another drip off my chin, my nose, draining life away. But more work needs to be done. Branches that sag with the weight of ripening fruit need to be staked or they will snap. Dead limbs need to be hauled out, so we drag them like corpses. Weeds grow wild, sapping moisture from the soil and our crops' roots, but our shovels bounce off the hardened earth when we try to dig them out.

Dad often told me that sweating hardens us. I thought that he meant that sweat was like the tough lessons of life. Now I know better. Hard sweat drains me of the moisture and resilience of youth. I've changed from a young farmer to an old one with nothing in between. My sweat drains from me as I give love to juicy peaches and sweet raisins.

I stagger home, take a long drink of water from our outdoor faucet. I turn, trudge up the steps to our farmhouse porch, and collapse, questioning if this is what farmers must do. Closing my eyes, I rest. I can hear myself breathing. One of our farm dogs, the golden retriever Jake, plops down near me. He sighs and shuts his eyes. I can feel my heart slowing and sense a hint of renewal. With luck, I'll nap for a few minutes, then stir and sit up, convincing myself I'm ready for more work.

Chapter Nineteen

THE HANDS OF CAREGIVERS

CAREGIVERS AND FARMERS share common ties. Both work long hours, often with little economic reward, and they labor in places where they have little control. They toil in obscurity, isolated and hidden from the public eye. Often, we only hear from them when they have to give bad news—a fall, a death, a stroke, a killing freeze that will result in food shortages and higher prices.

Hands that wash, lift, and clean. Wash, lift, and clean.
Wash, lift, and clean.

I watch my mother's hands grow old. My father's first major stroke is now eleven years ago, and another, more recent one now keeps him in a wheelchair. Eighty-six years old, Mom cares for him, making sure he doesn't fall, helping him clean up in the bathroom, monitoring his diet and medications—every morning, every evening, every day.

While Dad could be worse and his physical requirements much more demanding, Mom hasn't slept through the night in years, jumping up in a moment of panic whenever he stirs, fearing the worst, anticipating his needs. They face little daily challenges that drain both of them. I watch helplessly, accepting the reality that I can't change things for either of them.

Hands that bleed, crack, bruise, break, and heal. Callused hands.

Mom is part of an invisible corps of caregivers, a reliable army of workers who help others with their day-to-day needs, often in their homes. Some are professionals, such as occupational or physical therapists who work with those who have been injured. Most are relatives: a spouse caring for a loved one; a sister or brother assisting a sibling; children reversing roles to nurture and care for aging parents. The vast majority are women—wives and daughters who give up their lives to fill a need. Few are paid, their deeds often unnoticed. They labor quietly, asking little in return. They work because it's family.

Hands that know work. Hands that work together.

Mom and Dad worked this farm, sharing in the gamble of a young couple, dreaming of a place of their own. Their partnership was so common then on family farms that no one would have imagined it differently. As partners, together they lifted two-hundred-pound sweat boxes full of raisins. Mom laughs today, can't believe she did that, only possible with two people working well together, combining their strength.

The two of them had good timing, as the best partnerships do. As a kid, I drove the tractor on autumn afternoons, pulling the vineyard wagon down a row, with Mom on the wagon and Dad walking beside. As he reached down to pick up a paper tray of raisins that was rolled up like a cinnamon roll, he'd toss the four- or five-pound bundle up to the wagon. Mom would catch it midair, then stack it on the wagon bed, creating a pyramid, each roll interlocked with the one below and above, hundreds and hundreds of rolls fitting on a small wagon. With good timing, Dad did not need to stand fully with each toss, saving his back and muscles, blindly trusting Mom to catch and stack.

They filled one wagon and then another and another, often fifty in all, bringing in the harvest. The next day, while we kids were at school, they unrolled the trays, filled wooden boxes with the raisins, then stacked the heavy containers in a pile to be delivered weeks later. By the time I came home from school, the wagons were empty and ready to roll out again for more teamwork.

Hands that cook, mend, carry, and support. Hand labor.

Nothing in life prepared Mom for this. Suddenly she has been placed in a role of decision maker, trying to determine what's best for Dad. We try to work as family, all us kids supporting her, but like many caregivers, Mom feels odd delegating love, so she carries much of the burden herself.

I feel caught in the middle, too, part of the sandwich generation—raising my own children and now caring for aging parents. I share Mom's sense of responsibility, torn between others' needs and our own, balancing the needs of many. There is a tragic difference: I can see a future with our children, but Dad's future is short.

Hands that forgive. Hands that hope.

I once resented people who offer unsolicited advice without having experienced the daily realities of caregivers themselves. I used to get angry at peers who escaped this valley, leaving their parents and the task of caring for elderly people and farms to someone else. After watching my mother's heroics and other people's different lives, however, I understand that I need to accept their differences.

As in most families, not everyone gives the same. A son or daughter, a brother or sister may live far away and seem disconnected but may harbor guilt the rest of the family does not see. I'm not to judge. Mom once astutely said, "All those family dynamics don't bother me too much, I have enough to worry about."

The Hands of Caregivers

Wise hands. Understanding hands. Nurturing hands.

The fastest-growing segment of our nation's population is people over eighty-five. Our valley has an even higher number than average because so many young people have left the farms for the big city and many newcomers are retirees. Perhaps our agrarian roots give us an advantage: we know well the gradual pace of small-town life; we understand the meaning of those who plant roots. In our valley, as the elderly shift from a life of independence, we may be well positioned to adopt a culture of dependence in which we take pride in caring for one another.

Lost hands. Comforting hands. Hands that touch.

After his last stroke, I feared that Dad would miss farmwork and slip into a deep depression all the while peering out the back window of the house, trapped in his wheelchair, watching the farm change with the seasons, the peaches grow fat, the grapes lush. But something happened; the last major stroke in 2003 that sent him to the wheelchair also affected his mind. He now seems to live in a fog, a good fog that prevents him from thinking too much about what he can no longer do—the farmwork that remains, the chores incomplete, the unfinished business. Instead, he simply notices the change of seasons, the day-to-day activities he must do to function—time to eat, change clothes, time to sit and watch the farm change.

Now the natural fog on our farm—which helps peach trees slip into their deep sleep in winter and awaken in the spring after accumulating enough chilling hours—is also protecting Dad. Fog, the cold, damp chill of a winter morning that reduces sight and other senses, so that we become lost for hours in our own fields, becomes a friend. It becomes part of the caregiving world that envelops my father.

Hands that work, steer, guide, prune, shape, and renew. Hands that know the earth and respect the land.

Mom has simple goals now: waking up to take care of the little things; surviving daily; going to sleep at night hoping she did her best. On good days, she can slip back into her old life, shopping and doing town errands, making a special after-school snack for her grandson, or even taking a day off to go gambling and escape for a few hours. But the cares of caregivers quickly return, and they know the difference between their public lives and hidden, private realities.

Farming has helped me understand how to take care of things and live with nature. I learned of long-term commitment and unexpected results. Ironically—in a new age of information, high technology, and the rapid speed of change—a family-farm metaphor seems to work the best when caring for Dad, where things are slow, expectations humbling, and work fosters humility. Mom and Dad stayed put and grew old together, finding peace in a place called a farm.

Hands that worry. Hands that repair.

Mom worked alongside Dad for more than five decades. She witnessed the perfection he accomplished in his farm practices, his welding, his repairs. As his lifelong mate, she contributed to their perfect teamwork.

Now Dad will not get better. This is as good as he'll be. Mom's day-to-day situation is as good as it will get. But in her hands, Dad lives fully in the moment. I believe that he can only think about the immediate and is no longer burdened with the responsibility for others.

I now work alone—responsible for a farm, a family. I worry about my mom's hands, all our hands. My hands need to become bigger in order to embrace new worries and responsibilities.

Hands that hold. Hands that lead. Hands that dance.

I watch my mother prepare my father for sleep. They have a routine. First she pulls open the sheets and blanket, then helps position Dad, holding his side, shuffling her feet, guiding his. He pulls himself up out of the wheelchair and, with his good left hand, grabs hold of a metal bed support I welded together, utilizing pieces from our junk pile and grinding them smooth. The two twist and pivot like dancers. With a final turn, Dad heaves himself up and over, pausing as the couple break their embrace. Then he slowly sits, eventually landing on the bed. Mom lifts his legs, he turns to his side, shifts his weight, then rolls on his back. Mom leans over to tuck him in. He rests quietly, staring up at her. Mom gently smiles.

She is perfect in her care for him. This perfection is not noticed by the world, hidden in her day-to-day work, lost in the silence of Dad resting. Does she mind?

Familiar hands. Steady hands.

Working together, farm families are used to coping with rhythms of nature that don't always cooperate. They are used to flaws, stepping on one another's toes, making false turns, occasionally missing a leap and catch.

Mom and Dad, too, have learned how to ignore problems and redefine them as routines or mysteries. They start each new day knowing things may not get better, but they practice their teamwork and lose themselves in simple moments, when things feel right.

Slow hands. Constant hands. Hands we need.

Talking openly about aging makes many people feel uncomfortable. But growing old shouldn't be hidden, and caring should not be a secret. It's time we stop whispering about caregivers and honor them and their work.

Growing old can be lonely; our challenge is how we respond. Mom demonstrates her love and speaks loudly by her caring. She has permission to take some breaks, to get angry and depressed, to ask for face time with family members and not just phone calls. It's okay to ask for help and it's okay for her to be herself.

Hands that care. Hands that give.

Caregivers, all about giving and not receiving. So often the one you care for can't say thank you, can't express his gratitude, like Dad. Instead Mom works alone in a challenging partnership, sharing herself every day, often without receiving anything in return. Sometimes her acts are greeted with a look of confusion instead of a smile. But she continues, following another season of love.

Dad knows your hands, trusts your hands, loves your hands.

Chapter Twenty

FARMING WITH GHOSTS

LIKE MANY GOOD farmers, Dad had a great memory. He could recall harvests, disasters, and plantings. He remembered the details of a row of grapes planted a few inches closer together than other rows (and would drive the tractor and disc slower when working that row). He knew intimately the small, three-acre vineyard he pruned himself after his first stroke—slowly retraining it with stronger and better canes. During harvest, we see the results of his meticulous handiwork with slightly larger crops every year. He has left his mark on the land through his work.

I work with the ghosts of farmworkers past. They haunt me, mostly in the winter, when the tule fog hugs the earth for days. I trudge through the fields, forcing myself to venture into the wet, bone-chilling cold, listening to the moisture drip from the peach trees and grapevines. That's when the ghosts greet me: a shadow in the gray mist, something familiar in the distance, moving methodically among the grapevines, a fellow worker lost in the white glare of winter.

Our family were not always farmers, but we have all been farmworkers. Dad and Mom and my jiichan and baachan—all started in the fields. Part of an army of common laborers, immigrant workers collectively changed our valley's natural desert into a garden. Those ghosts leveled the uneven earth, planted trees and vines, hauled out hardpan from fields, dug out the Johnson grass that bound up the soil of poor lands, brought fertility to barren soil in exchange for cheap wages that enabled others to prosper.

An irrigation ditch borders our farm. It was hand dug by farmworkers in the early 1900s, using a Fresno scraper, an earth-moving and leveling implement pulled behind horses and mules. Teams of men moved dirt, dug canals, and graded a channel for water to be diverted from the Kings River, which flows west to us from its origins high in the Sierra Nevada. The channel spreads across miles and miles of farmland. Our ditch, the Fowler Switch, is one branch, journeying ten miles from the river, snaking through the countryside, so that farms on either side of the channel have access to its life-giving water. Our man-made "river" gently slopes from the head gate and brings us water for months during the heat of summer, an amazing engineering feat considering the lack of tractors and bulldozers a hundred years ago. Only with a legion of strong backs could these waterways have been carved out of the parched desert landscape. I remember these laborers' ghosts whenever I walk our land.

Some of our vines are close to one hundred years old, planted by immigrants when they were new to the area, pruned by Japanese Americans, possibly even my grandmother and grandfather. Near the irrigation ditch, these old vines bend over more than they stand, trunks gnarled and twisted after decades of growth, showing the wear from years of their own work and hinting at the shapes of the ghosts of old workers who cared for them.

As common laborers, not landowners, these workers were invisible. They had no names. Many, like Dad, carried a dream of progressing from laborer to owner, of becoming a farmer. Then as now, farmers and workers looked similar working in the fields, both hunched over with hoe or shovel in the blistering heat of summer or huddled around a small fire at the edge of a vineyard in the middle of winter, trying to get feeling back into fingers and hands before returning to pruning. When Dad first returned to these fields after Relocation, he and his parents would prune a neighbor's orchard and vineyard to earn cash, then come home late in the day or at the end of the season to work on our own rented place. Later, when Dad became the farmer and hired help, he worked side by side with the pruners and pickers. He treated them with respect because he was once one of them. A Latino friend who also grew up in the fields respected those farmers who worked with their crews, everyone sharing the dust and taste of sweat as class lines blurred.

Dad also worked with ghosts. As a child, I watched him come in from a long, long day in the fields. He'd pulled off his gloves and set them on a workbench; I'd witness them gradually opening, slowly relaxing, as if life were escaping. Sometimes I tried them on, and my hands had to conform to the bent fingers, the leather stiff and rough from dried sweat. I could not escape the hours of labor beat into those gloves and had trouble imagining that I could fill those gloves.

Do these things still matter? If you believe in ghosts, they do.

Farmworkers have left their marks on all the vines, pruning scars from generations that helped shape our farm. A good year can mean more work as additional acres are planted. In the past, farmers expanded their holdings, plowing profits back into the land, creating more work, more jobs. Prosperity here does seem to trickle down to all, my family benefiting from a growing valley and contributing to its growth.

I can still see the vines I pruned as a restless teenager, impatient with life here on the farm, anticipating the excitement of living in a new world beyond the mountains. Because of my lack of focus, when Dad showed me how to prune a grapevine, he gave me the worst and hardest to prune. "Why have a beginning pruner destroy a perfectly good vine?" was his rationale.

He was right. I'd chop up the vine, leaving some canes too long, cutting spurs back too much, never quite understanding how to generate the best crop along with stimulating canes for next year and the year after that. Now, forty years later, I regret my behavior and of course wish I had been more patient. I must live with these skeletons from my past. It takes years to nurture the weak back to health.

Baachan died more than ten years ago, her mind failing long before her muscles. Physically she was hardened from years of battling Johnson grass. I remember her carrying a shovel over her shoulder and shuffling out into the fields to do battle with this evil weed, preventing it from becoming established. In the evening, she'd come home, quietly store the shovel, and come in for dinner. No one knew where she had been all day, but when driving through the fields, I would see evidence of her work. By each small pile of dead weeds where she had shoveled, she left part of herself.

As I walk our farm today, especially during the last light of day, I occasionally see a dark shadow trudging down a dirt avenue or slouching over on the horizon along the ditch bank. I think it's her spirit, still walking lands she worked but never owned; the lost soul of a field-worker who never grew rich while the land grew fat with harvests . . . searching, but never fulfilled.

The ghosts of today's farmworkers haunt my fields, only a few ever able to move up from field hand to owner. Few of today's workers have dreams of farming here in California, because the price of land, the capital investment required, and the larger and larger economies of scale create barriers to ownership. A few workers have places of their own in Mexico, but most come here in search of a job. They're another wave of labor from a foreign land, paid to grow our foods and stay in the shadows. As the farmer who hires them, I try to be a boss but not an exploiter.

The working conditions remain gruesome, our twenty-one days in a row of record heat over one hundred degrees in summer 2008—right in the middle of our peach harvest—a painful reminder of farming's reality. Ripe peaches don't wait for pleasant days; nature dictates the working conditions. Yet workers come, sweat, and take home money. Many send their earnings back to their homes. Our little country post office annually ships millions of dollars in money orders to small, rural villages in remote areas of Mexico alone. Our valley in California supports another valley thousands of miles away.

In our country, we have a cheap-food policy—a trend that hasn't changed from Dad's farming days to mine. Americans spend less on food than any other nation in the world. Every year farmers try to grow more efficiently and more productively, chasing after the fewer and fewer dollars that the public is willing to spend. All the while, we face more and more competition. At the mercy of the marketplace, we grow a product, commit our labor, and pay up front with no idea of the price we will receive. There are no futures markets with fruits and vegetables. Paying more for labor is not simply an expense that farmers can pass on to the consumer.

Today, we are losing our farmlands. Drive around our valley and you will see another vineyard pulled out, grapes yanked from the earth, roots ripped from our valley, vines that can produce heavy harvests but whose prices no longer support the effort. Each block of vines, a small forty-acre farm with the farmer probably in his sixties or seventies, is land that now sits idle. Crop prices are so bad that farmers no longer even know what to plant instead of grapes. This is a relatively new development. Farmers never used to leave fields empty. Invisible are the lost wages of a farmworker who could have pruned, irrigated, weeded, and harvested: tens of thousands of dollars in wages ripped from our local economy for each of these lost farms, money never earned.

Perhaps the ghosts of today's farmers and workers haven't changed that much from those of the past. Both are caught in a system that beats us down with physical work, risks, and vulnerability, without the potential for huge rewards. In these thoughts, I come face-to-face with a cold, gripping reality: my own mortality. Can a farm live on while the farmer and worker die?

There are no quick solutions to the farming crisis. Rarely do the unseen garner attention. Local leaders focus on attracting new industry and better-paying jobs, forgetting our agrarian roots and family farms, even though they still comprise a multibillion-dollar industry that generates well-paying, skilled jobs. But agriculture is still supported on the backs of low-wage earners. The ghosts who help grow our food will always be around. Wishing they'd go away will only drive them from our valley into another country, which would be our own loss as a nation. Yet many seem to find comfort in keeping the invisible invisible.

I dream of improving working conditions on our small farm and offering better-paying jobs. The living-wage movement—which wants to pay workers more than minimum wages so they can move beyond poverty—is trying to establish a new economy based on the full worth of people's labor, one that does not simply try to pay the least. It has made inroads in the coffee industry, creating Fair Trade coffee, a branded product for which consumers often pay more, knowing that the people who grow the coffee and work the fields are getting a living wage.

I believe that we can have fair trade with progressive peaches or radical raisins, an agriculture driven by consumers who are willing to pay more because they know the story of their food and know that paying pennies more per pound rewards those who work the land. After all, feel-good economics is what's at the soul of food. We eat to feel good. I believe that this is possible, but I haven't figured out how to make it happen. Because I have no answer, I have been criticized. Some critics scoff at my fair-trade idealism, but those skeptics haven't worked around the invisible lately.

One step I have taken is to start a very small program of giving a few bonuses to our workers. When we presented our first checks, we were met with confused looks. They did not understand why we were giving them money. My Spanish is poor, so I had trouble explaining the payment. Sadly, I realized I had never used the word *bonus* with our workers. Even sadder, they had never received a bonus before. We searched for the right term. Fittingly, we call it *gratificación*. It was our small tribute to ghosts.

The ghosts of past, present, and future stay with me in the fields. Perhaps my calling is to tell a tale of workers on the land and the story of the silent hands and unseen faces behind our foods. One day, I, too, will become nameless. I, too, will become nothing. But the marks that I have left on my land and on family and coworkers may still be in evidence.

Chapter Twenty-one

MISSING STORIES

A QUIET, RESERVED FARMER, Dad was not a natural storyteller, more comfortable with trees and vines as companions and with a shovel or pruning shear in his hands. He rarely told tales or offered unsolicited opinions and observations. Sometimes I wished we were like the Hawaiians I had met with their "talk story," or Southerners with their long, embroidered tales.

When I first came back to the farm after college, Dad and I had months of lunches together, just him and me, taking a break between our morning and afternoon work sessions. We'd talk, but it usually began with my questions.

"Tell me again, why do the grapes struggle in our youngest vineyard?" I'd prompt.

"It was where they once planted cotton," Dad answered.

Cotton was grown not only in the South but also in the dry, empty fields on the west side of our valley.

"I picked cotton a few years," Dad added.

I hadn't thought many Japanese Americans worked in cotton fields, but Dad would not elaborate that day. We talked about the weather, the farmwork to be done, but nothing more about cotton until the next day.

"Cotton?" I asked, again, and Dad told of farmers growing it as a cash crop, an annual planting to tide them over while their perennial vines or trees grew. Japanese and Mexican immigrants, with long bags trailing behind them, picked the fiber and earned some money.

Over a few days, Dad filled in the missing facts in that story.

"Cotton is hard on the land: it takes a lot out of it. That's why the vines will struggle—until we build up the soil," Dad added.

Finally, I had the whole story and through it the answer to my question. Over the next series of lunches we talked about other fields, and I renamed them, marking them on a farm map, adding a sense of history to the farm. That's how our Cotton Block was named, along with the Hardpan hill (the highest area on the farm), the Riffel field (the name of the former owner), and the Suns (where a Sun Grand nectarine once grew).

Eventually the whole farm's story was retold and mapped.

I tell stories. I can't help but see the world through stories, listening to people talk about their home places, feeling the emotions of everyday situations. Before his stroke, Dad and I talked a lot, although I did most of the talking. He was an excellent listener. We talked during work, lunch, coffee breaks, rainy days, foggy mornings, after work, while resting during a break, in between repairing equipment while welding, as we loaded or unloaded boxes, picked peaches, or boxed raisins. Often some of our best discussions were in the fields or in the shed, under a truck hood or in the shade of a tree as we repaired a tractor, between welds and acetylene cuts, changing discs or flat furrows, hooking up wagons or planters or drills.

Rarely did we just talk. Often his stories were triggered by an object, an artifact from the past or a tool of the present. He'd show me a technique, or we'd go out into the fields to practice squeezing dirt to measure water content or to discover how deep a weed root penetrated.

Often with Dad, I thought out loud. I may have helped to provide some entertainment during a typical workday. He'd offer a few of his own thoughts or a response. I believe he enjoyed the company.

Since he lost his ability to speak, of course, the stories have changed. A few times he managed to convey an idea through a few scribbled words on a paper. Once, he scrawled the letters O-S-T-I-C on a paper and pointed to the fields. This confused us all—Mom, Marcy, even the kids all tried to decipher the meaning. We thought Dad was confused as we tried various letter combinations, attempting to decipher his message. Only later that evening, when we got a call from a neighbor, did we solve the word-jumble. Kay phoned and asked, "I know this sounds odd, but did you lose an ostrich? Believe it or not, I was driving up our driveway and saw one wandering in your fields!" Mystery solved.

Other times I would interview Dad with question after question and he would respond with a nod yes or no. We communicated in fragments. Sadly, Dad has stories we'll never know.

Marcy now is my main listener; she hears my thoughts and stories. I suppose this is part of becoming a life partner, a soul mate. My stories need "talking out"—at an early stage they need an audience who simply listens. Some days work wonderfully—my thoughts are coherent, I can express myself with authenticity, the stories are real and contain a universal truth. Often ideas need to be thought through and some developed further. But stories help me learn to farm. I never studied agriculture and failed to take a single class in college dealing with agricultural sciences. I learned by osmosis and observation while growing up and then returning to work the farm. My learning curves were gradual, but the process of thinking through situations, challenges, and experiments was fun and engaging. That's why I also write journals—to continue to try to work things out. Thoughts of Dad often fill my pages, because I miss our talks and stories.

Immediately following Dad's stroke I stayed away from his tractor. It reminded me of how I had found him, wandering around in a daze, confused and in pain while the engine roared. The tractor sat unused until I finally realized that I needed to start it occasionally, to keep the battery charged and find out if there was indeed some other problem it had that Dad had been trying to solve.

It started fine. But because less than a week had passed since Dad's stroke, I wasn't ready to take it back out into the fields. At that point, we still weren't sure whether or not he would recover and wake up from his coma. Besides, I had other tractors I could use. I removed the key and opened the toolbox attached to the tractor frame, alongside the engine, to store the key inside.

Inside the box I discovered three shiny oranges, still fresh. Dad had picked them from our lone tree, waiting until the end of winter when they were very sweet. He had packed them on the tractor so that he could have a snack during a break in the fields. He enjoyed his work so much that he took treats with him, not wanting to take the time to drive back to the house for respite. He took comfort in the fields, drawing no lines between rest and work.

Later that day I brought the family to the shed to show my discovery in the toolbox. As we walked there, Marcy was quietly talking about preparing for the worst with Dad; we were not sure the kids had black clothes. When I opened the toolbox, the bright oranges stood vivid against the gray engine and the faded red engine bonnet.

Having spent a week in the hospital, worrying and wondering, we were overwhelmed with grief and depression. The story of Dad's having the oranges, of planning his indulgence, a moment of happiness in the fields, made us smile and reflect. His memory would always be with us. Then I stopped talking and wept. Marcy hugged me; the rest of the family joined.

Nikiko would never forget that act of her grandfather. Korio, only six at the time, remembers the scene, too. Marcy reminds me how sweet the oranges would have been at that time of year.

We didn't eat those oranges but left them in the toolbox, hoping Dad would come home soon to find them himself. And if Dad didn't come home, I knew I'd find them later and have this tangible memory of him.

That night, I wrote about oranges and Dad's missing stories in my journal. Writing the phrase "I will miss Dad" was both emotionally difficult and yet liberating. I admitted that I would miss him. I confronted the loss of my father, the changes that I would have to live with, that he, if he survived, would have to live with.

I carry mental maps of our farm along with its landmarks in the history of our family. As I personalize our farm, I leave behind the imprint of stories, like oranges in a toolbox, or the effect of dynamite on hardpan, the crooked rows of trees I planted, and the irrigation valve that leans to the left, slightly off balance, forever marking where I began to learn the art of working with cement. I think of my uncle Alan when I use one particular tractor. After he passed away, I purchased his Ford tractor, a low-profile model that fits under trees, perfect for our fields, on which we can crouch and lean to one side, dodging low-hanging branches. But it was the farm auction after he died that I recall the most when I use that tractor, the awkward feeling of walking through Uncle Alan's barnyard, of other farmers going through his farm remains, his stories, whispering quietly. I wanted to shout out and let them know who this farmer was and the meaning of his equipment. I wanted to tell the story behind the buck rake that both he and my dad once used, that they repaired and welded whenever it broke—it still bears those scars. I want to explain why Uncle had those oxyacetylene tanks that he had purchased but never used, instead coming over to visit with Dad to share the repair project, a rare partnership between siblings. But I didn't need to. Most of these older farmers understood the meaning of such an estate sale. We all sensed our own mortality.

Here, too, is the exact field where Marcy first met Dad. She and I were working in a vineyard, planting runners and replacing missing vines by pulling a cane from a mature vine and burying it in the dirt. In a few years, a new vine would grow from this planting. It resembled an umbilical cord, a mother plant growing a baby next to it. When Dad saw the two of us in the vineyard, he approached, smiled, and said hello. I introduced Marcy—mud on her pants, dirt in her hair, dust coating her face. After Dad left, she sighed, "I look a mess."

As we move on, we leave behind our stories in interior and exterior landscapes. The looming fog of death, the passing of time, the nature of change all lead us to greater self-awareness, and to a final transformation. We mourn the loss of our people and miss them. But we continue to tell their stories.

Chapter Twenty-two

FIELDS OF GOLD

I FARM WITH GOURMET dust. I breathe it, I eat it; it has become part of me and I part of it. I am blessed to have such fine dust.

Farm dust varies with soil types and regions. The Northeast has its glacial till, which drives farmers crazy, more boulders than dirt, topsoil washing away with rains. The Great Plains soil holds centuries of prairie grass blended into a rich, fertile land, its dust offering an earthy aroma. Georgia's red clay carries a legendary taste of sharp minerals, and Wisconsin dairy lands and Washington's Skagit Valley, with their rains and lush growth, have a heavy dust with a thick, rich quality, like a fattening chocolate dessert.

My dust is a fine powder and a chef's delight. Add water to my soil and create a rich roux, thick but workable. Stir it and the air will fill with the rich aroma of turned earth. Beat the ground with a disc and a fine meal is created. Just as bakers have flour, farmers have topsoil. In fact, my topsoil is like sifted flour, awaiting further ingredients to take on beautiful forms and flavors.

Generations of farmers have tasted this flavor in fruit that is seasoned with a certain tang. For decades we have licked our lips when working in this dust to grow juicy grapes and peaches. The dust tempers the character of our fruits: peaches are sweet but not like candy, grapes are delicate, light in their bursts of juice. Dad and I cannot take a bite from one of our peaches or eat one of our grapes without tasting this dust. It's our communion.

Autumn marks the end and a beginning. The summer peach harvests are complete, the leaves in their final month of work before they begin to yellow and fall and the tree takes its rest. Some leaves have been busy since March, laboring through three seasons to produce a fat harvest. In October they turn bright yellow, orange, and scarlet. They complete the valley's canvas, vivid against distant gray mountains and browning fields and still-green vineyards. As they begin to drift to the ground, both the branches and the earth share their colors for a few weeks.

In the late fall, the grapes, which hang on to their leaves until a bitter frost, begin to relax. By November some turn yellow, others sag and seem to concede the end is near but refuse to fall. They will then turn brown, withering on the vine before dropping to the earth.

Dad loved driving the tractor at this time of the year. For most farmers, the pressures of the harvest are over, the stress of decision making and management done. They can relax, responsibilities completed for a time. They make a final pass over the land, preparing it for spring, reflecting on the past and planning for the future.

On our farm, we rarely have rains in the late summer and early fall. Occasionally October has a few showers. We may apply a final irrigation, adding water to root zones, a final sip before winter rains. But the ground quickly dries out, weeds shrivel, even Johnson grass begins to brown. Our sandy loam soil becomes parched, returning to its original desert form.

We finish the year in clouds of dust. Driving down avenues, a swirl of dust follows all movement. Walking creates little puffs around our legs. Our dog, an especially old one, loves to run in this soft earth and create a trail of dust behind her, a column suspended in her wake, giving the illusion of speed.

In the autumn before Dad lost his mobility to another stroke,

I asked him to make a final pass with the tractor and disc in order to knock down the weeds one last time, to level the earth for winter. He drove for hours, a tan statue mounted on the tractor, a fine layer of dirt coating his skin and clothing, his work completed with a baptism of dust.

Lost in his work, alive, happy, he went up and down the rows. The air was still, so I could determine his location by the cloud of dust curling behind him. He worked long that day, and, in the evening, drove the tractor into the yard, knowing that it needed diesel for the next day.

As he carefully climbed down from the seat, an eighty-two-year-old Pig-Pen from a Peanuts cartoon, dust billowed around his feet and hands, a constant swirling companion with each movement. His hat was tan with particles, clothes and face streaked with dirt. Any horizontal part of him—his shoulders, his lap, even the tops of his hands as he held the steering wheel—were dust repositories. His usually white hair stuck out from beneath his oval straw work hat, tinted with dust to an unnaturally light brown. Even his eyelashes had a veil of dust on them, and when he blinked, puffs danced in front of his eyes.

I patted him on the back, sending another blast of dust airborne. My taps changed to flaps as I tried to whisk it away, but we became enveloped by the dust. I squatted and worked over his legs, his thighs heavy with dirt, and shook loose what seemed to be a few pounds, which piled around his shoes. Dad was proud of the dust, having worked a full day, the elderly farmer proving his worth. He was still valued, old but not obsolete.

As I tried to dust off his hair, he bowed slightly, lowered his head, then dipped his knees, almost a genuflection. He closed his eyes and puffs of dust scattered as I gently rubbed his head, massaging and cleansing. He looked content, as if thanking me for my care, my benediction on his good work. On his face, an impish grin grew. Dust and all, this was Dad. And this dust is me, too.

My old pickup doesn't drive fast, more comfortable in first gear than overdrive, and forces me to set aside any impatience I may have. It likes to mosey along, keeping down the dust, which trees and vines do not like. Dust coats their leaves and slows their growth; thick layers also promote the growth of mites that suck the life out of green tissue. Fortunately, the dust season comes in autumn, toward the end of their cycle.

When I work for hours in the fields, my journey is often circular: I may drive a tractor down a quarter-mile row, turn ten yards, and drive up the neighboring row, back nearly to where I started. Depending on the wind currents, I'll often pass through the dust I create. The faster I drive, the more dust I breathe during my return trip. There is no escape, dust is everywhere.

In the late afternoon especially, dust becomes my companion. The cool evening air presses down the warm air of the daytime, creating a still, lifeless atmosphere. As I walk, puffs of dust from my boots linger and collect. I can look behind me and see my trail floating in the air.

One evening after a long workday, I visit with Dad. He, too, is tired but smiles the way I do after a hard day's work. He has washed up and is relaxing before dinner. We talk, then I head back out, taking advantage of the remaining light. Dad nods approval, knowing you sometimes start another day with the evening sun in order to catch up on chores.

The autumn sunset sits gloriously on the horizon, the final light reflecting rays through some clouds; brilliant orange and purple color the sky. The day is done. The trees and vines still carry autumn's yellow and brown hues, fallen leaves blanket the earth. The fields are golden.

I'm preparing for a final irrigation by setting the water valves with a few quick turns. When Dad worked late, I thought he was sacrificing his time and himself for his family, logging long hours as if working a double shift, saving the expense of hiring someone else. Now I realize that we work until the sun sets because we are in sync with the day. It's not about production but being productive with a natural work rhythm: working with nature, alone, by yourself.

The history of Dad's work lingers like the dust behind me. Now I do what he once did, slow, methodical. Not a march, but a pace that feels like it will continue forever. Part of a long line of farmers during their evening walks, now I'm also part of something more.

When we lose our fathers we can lose this rhythm. When our fathers are gone we miss their dust. Then we find our own pace and tempo and we create our own trails.

The meaning of Dad is found in these fields. He would want us to judge him by his works—the work seen in the land. As I walk these lands, the farm becomes the father, imbued with ghosts. Walking these fields of gold, as often as I do this, I will think of Dad.

Part Five

Succession

Chapter Twenty-three

PLACES WHERE WE BELONG

When in her eighties, Baachan began to show symptoms of dementia and the early stages of Alzheimer's. But on the farm, because she had her own routine and work, her confusion was masked. We did not notice the times she became disoriented or lost track of where she was while shoveling weeds. In perhaps a wonderful way, it simply did not matter: we had plenty of weeds.

As time passed, she wandered more, traveling down the dirt avenues, simply walking. One day, she saw me with my shovel over my shoulders and asked who I was, where I was going, and what work I was doing. This had happened occasionally for a few months, but then it became more frequent. Once or twice a week she did not recognize me and wanted to know where I was going and what work there was to do.

I finally asked her, "Where are you going?" She didn't answer directly, instead started singing a simple song.

I was startled. My grandmother had never sung before. The tiny, four-foot-nine-inch woman hunched before me seemed content, her voice pleasant. I asked what song she was singing.

She said it was a nursery rhyme. Didn't I know it? All the country children in Japan knew it.

In her old age, my grandmother's memory was changing. She'd revisit her childhood in the small village of Takamura outside

Kumamoto in southern Japan. As she walked our avenues, she retraced the paths that had crisscrossed the ancient rice fields of her native land, journeying back and forth from the small country school not too far from their home in the village.

Her memory blended the past with the present and I became just another villager walking to his farm for a day's work. She was a child, free of the burden of adult work, completing her morning chores and walking to school, singing. The time was possibly in the early 1900s, before her father had died young, and she was about ten or eleven. The oldest child, she would be forced to quit school to work the fields. Later, when her younger brother, the oldest son in the household, finished high school and could take over the farm, she was displaced. She then became a picture bride, two families arranging a marriage by exchanging photographs. Her match, my grandfather, was twenty years older and had already journeyed to America. My grandmother left her family farm to join him and a life of hard work.

But while walking our fields, Baachan was lost in memories of a happy moment in her hard life—before the harsh years of farming and life in a foreign land where she'd always been treated as an alien. During her walks, singing to herself, drifting into stories from her childhood, she found a place where she belonged.

Now I know why, as long as he was mobile, Dad was the first to go out to prune the vineyards every year. For a farmer, it was a ritual, a recognition of nature's cycle of life, a rite of passage from one year to the next. In his eightieth season, he was also revisiting old friends in his pruning. Our Thompson grapes had been planted in 1918, four years before he was even born; I suppose it was rejuvenating to work with something always older than himself. If the vines could be productive year after year, so could he.

A sojourner, Dad lived temporarily in the vineyards one day, then moved to another field the next, as did the many migrants who had lived and worked in these fields, farmworkers and generations of immigrants. Relocation during World War II altered the natural cycle. Nisei, though American born, were displaced along with their immigrant parents. Forced to become sojourners, they bore the scars of being uprooted; some, like Dad, carried the burden more than others—he was affected by the distrust and fear my baachan carried, a quiet whisper and a very subtle but lingering doubt that questioned whether he belonged in America.

Nonetheless, Dad believed in America and called himself American. During the civil rights struggles of the 1960s, he often told us that he understood what it was like to be treated differently. But rather than support the protesters, he became the invisible man, heading out into the fields in the darkness of morning, working in the sunlight of the long day, and eventually returning in the evening whole.

My sansei generation was brought up very American. Typical of immigrant family histories, we grew disconnected from our family's homeland and speak very little Japanese. Many grew up never talking with their grandparents; we were sent off to college. Those from farm families participated in our own evacuation and exodus from rural communities. We created our own diaspora. We lost the language of home and heritage.

Farmers often talk to themselves, part of a rhythm of working alone. As we get older, we grow so accustomed to the isolation that, when others are around, we may forget we have an audience. Once I listened to an old farmer talk out loud to himself, then, when his farm dog accompanied him, he grew very expressive and even emotional. He spoke tenderly to the creature, petted him, and talked as the black tail wagged back and forth and the red tongue licked his hand. He loved the dog. Yet when I saw the same farmer at home with his wife who was ill and not expected to improve, he grew withdrawn and very quiet. He didn't know what to say to her or how to talk with her. Later, as he and I walked the fields, I asked about his wife and her condition. He grew quiet then whispered, "I didn't expect she would die first."

With pruning shears ready, Dad paused to examine a vine, talking to himself, trying to discover the history and listen to the story in each living creature. The vines wait patiently during their annual haircut, already resting deep in their winter dormancy. In the coarse, gnarled black bark of a twisted, contorted ancient trunk, he finds pruning scars from prior generations. Had he left these wounds a decade ago—or was it two?—when he decided to reshape the vine radically, the crown already growing too far from the stake, making it lopsided. He had cut off half, giving up part of a harvest that season, but a healthy vine now hugs the stake, strong, balanced. Dad knew the secret of sacrifice.

Good pruning is really the art of taking away, like a sculptor chiseling at a rock, working to uncover life inside. Dad paced around the grapevine, paused and clipped, leaning in and cutting; eyes darting back and forth, searching for the strong canes, locating spurs for next year's growth. He worked with the past and saw the future—adding to a living timeline.

The dialogue between farmer and vine must be slow and engaging. It takes time to get to know a vine, to pay attention to the nuances. A farmer's relationship with the land grows by gradual accrual, punctuated by the annual rites of pruning, watering, and harvesting. I've discovered a secret that Dad knew for years: we work with the intention of returning the next year and the year after that. Imagine how much better the world would be if we all grew relationships with such intentions.

Farmers must talk to their vines and trees; as I've said, on many days these plants are our only companions. Our twenty- or forty-acre plots separate us from neighbors. Should we come across another soul working in another field or passing by along the roadside, we communicate by waves, since shouts may not be heard, an art form that Dad taught by example.

The wave: the arm is raised slowly, allowing for recognition despite the distance. A dramatic reaching for the sky, a single hand stretches upward, fingers open. Hold it upright until seen and greeted with a like response, the space between two people shrinking with each second. Then each turns to his separate field for another pass down a row, workers disappearing back into the landscape.

Over a field, across an irrigation ditch, from opposite sides of a dirt avenue, a wave becomes the common language of place. The wave, a moment of recognition between two individuals, each saying, "You matter."

When I wave, I expect a wave back. A genuine wave, like a solid handshake, can overcome many differences. As our valley grows and its populations change, we now most often wave to non-English speakers. Our lack of a common language matters little. We are joined by a working-class bond, our waving an act of public recognition. We acknowledge each other with a wave, a visible sign proclaiming that the other exists. I find that comforting, something that builds community and creates neighbors. Go to a place where people don't care for one another, and you won't see waves.

We're losing the art of physical communication. In a high-tech world, the wave gives way to a text message, lost amid two hundred downloads. A digital revolution requires less reading of body language and more scanning of emails and blogs. People pay less attention to the immediate physical world and focus more attention on the virtual world.

So, is my wave a relic of a dying, old-world culture, a remnant of traditions that no longer have a place? With maturity, I have discovered the need for more waves. Old folks, because of their declining eyesight and hearing, rely more on touch, handshakes, and hugs, which mean a lot.

Most of the time, Dad and I labor alone, independent of others, protected from the rest of the world, safe and secure with our companions. Gardeners must feel the same when they retreat to their backyard beds, speaking with flowers, cajoling the buds, or cursing the weeds. I talk with my vines now, too, like visiting a cemetery and talking with neighbors who have passed on, only these plants and fields are still alive. Usually I first ask how they feel and I make a request—please warn me if there's a problem with mildew, worms, or a short crop. The grapes dangle quietly, and if I'm lucky, the leaves respond with a rustle.

I'm fortunate that I have touchstones to nature and her seasons through history and my family, the land and the memories. Fortune surrounds us partly because we've stayed put. As change churns and swirls around our farm, the real and authentic become more important. Dad and I remain in concert with the land, developing relationships with our vines and trees, creating a place where the world can come to us. We belong to this place and it belongs to us.

I look at old farmers out early each winter, trudging into fields with shears in hand. Snip, cut, slice. Vine after vine. They prune a little each day, keeping themselves busy, I suppose, and witness daily accomplishments with a sense of productivity. They look content. By pruning each winter, they speak clearly: they intend to see the grapes all the way through one more summer and one more harvest.

Chapter Twenty-four

HOW MANY HARVESTS LEFT?

BEFORE DAD SUFFERED his stroke, I did not worry about my future as a farmer. So long as a parent stands in front of you, a buffer between you and death, you don't think much about your own death. You are not the next in line. Following Dad's stroke, this changed.

Over morning coffee, I talk with Marcy about plans to plant another heirloom peach variety and where on the farm it would grow best. She pauses and asks, "How many harvests do you have left?"

The question stuns me. Up to that point, I had not measured my life in prospective harvests. I remember all my harvests past but never thought to calculate my remaining years. That implies a finite number.

The idea of "my years left" was a wake-up call. You can do a lot with ten more harvests and perhaps twice as much with twenty. Yet upon closer examination, even twenty more harvests is not that long. A newly planted orchard takes four to five years to produce its first substantial harvest. That leaves fifteen more harvests. Figure that in at least a few of those years, things won't go well—you'll have a late winter frost, heavy spring rain on blossoms that keeps them from setting fruit and breeds brown rot, lousy market prices, labor shortages—

or a personal screwup that hurts the crop. Subtract three or four bad harvests and that leaves only about a dozen more.

A dozen more harvests in my life—the thought makes me pause and take stock. Quantifying my life scares me. I can hear a bell tolling over my fields and it sends a shiver down my back.

Dad once advised me: "Don't count too much at harvest time." He meant not to add up your profits too soon—it was bad luck and you'd probably be disappointed. It's like saying, "Don't count your chickens before they're hatched," which I rarely hear anymore—chickens and rural life are so alien to most people today. But it is still a wise approach to peaches, as well as to stock yields and retirement accounts.

At harvest, we have a general sense of the market prices and we do contemplate stopping the work if the picking and pricing don't add up. Yet even if we face terrible prices, a ripe peach or sweet grape demands to be picked. We have no choice.

As my parents often said, *Shikata ga nai*—it can't be helped—a principle that does actually help me to cope with the whims of nature. Yet I wonder if this belief also makes me hesitant to forge ahead with new enterprises and fearful of failing.

Dad taught me another, similar phase that also translates into "it can't be helped"—*Sho ga nai*. It took years for me to understand the context for when to use this phrase. *Sho ga nai* is less formal than *Shikata ga nai* (although others often use the two interchangeably), more conversational, much like the French saying *C'est la vie* or the Spanish, *Así es la vida*. When life throws you a curve, you accept the unpleasant situation—you're powerless to avoid it or make changes. *Sho ga nai* says that we acknowledge life and respond accordingly. It does not mean "I can't be bothered" or "it doesn't matter" or "I don't care." (The ultimate expression of *Sho ga nai* was used by the emperor of Japan at the end of World War II when he asked his people to embrace defeat.) Dad used the more formal *Shikata ga nai* when talking about Relocation; it was a wound for him that brought public shame, public humiliation—it was formal and not just personal.

Every harvest, I think of Dad's advice about not "counting" and try to avoid disappointment. But I believe that I can balance the legacy of realism and resignation with my own optimism and desire to improve, to change the farm for the better, even in the face of some inevitable setbacks. It is in my power to plan and to plant a beautiful new orchard even though market and weather effects on it are beyond my control. And I love to plant a beautiful heirloom peach orchard. I take it all personally. *Sho ga nai.*

My father may also have thought about timelines and lifespans, as his announcement about planting his last orchard would indicate. All farmers follow seasonal rhythms, a calendar in sync with nature. Many stretch their personal and professional calendars into years and decades, especially those who grow perennial crops such as orchards and vineyards.

So far my timelines have been shorter, often measured by my work boots, which last for two or three years before they fall apart completely. The leather cracks, the heels grind down unevenly, the stitching frays and breaks. They are exhausted. The soles on one pair split apart after I abused them by walking over a burn pile that had hidden embers. Even duct tape cannot extend the seasons of my boots. Eventually I toss them into a box from which they rarely resurface. After decades of working together, Dad and I could line up all our old boots side by side but can no longer tell the difference between his and mine.

It's still unclear whether my own children, Nikiko and Korio, will follow in our boot steps on the farm. Nikiko, now twenty-three, thinks of coming home to the farm; while at seventeen and still in high school, Korio isn't sure what he wants to do. He's much more relaxed than his sister and helps me out, but when asked about the future of our farm, he answers, "I'll help my sister." He doesn't want to disappoint Marcy and me, though, and naturally puts himself second, like a second son. Even with their intelligence and hard work, however, my children may find they are not suited to becoming farmers. In the new century, farming will necessitate something beyond the ethic of working hard. What it will require remains a mystery, which will become evident only as the century unfolds.

I'd like to pass on to my children the art of listening, of hearing the unspoken needs of plants and people, which is required to learn how to farm. Like keeping old work boots, farmers need to carry baggage that reminds them of lessons from the past that they gleaned by being dedicated to their harvests.

I once asked Dad when he would know it was time to stop farming.

He said, "I wouldn't want to know."

Like Dad, I have never thought about retiring either. I have no artificial date by which my farm's work ends. I will stop when I can no longer work.

Sadly, I will have no final instruction from Dad. Final lectures happen only when you know you're going away and want an official end to one life phase at the beginning of another. Dad lives with an awareness of his mortality and yet without awareness of when this next phase of his life will end. Not knowing how many harvests I have left may help me live more wisely. I can still work with hope: hope that there is a future I can contribute to; hope that I can still leave behind significance; hope that sustains me into the future, because part of the future is yet to be created.

Others who love what they do share this perspective. Committed teachers continue to teach after retirement even after their last full-time harvest of students. Many continue to work as grandparents or in their communities. Their students change, as do their teaching methods, but good educators keep educating. Health professionals don't stop caring for others on receipt of their first Social Security check. Blue-collar workers don't stop working with their hands. With retirement, the hours may be different, the work settings change, but staying active keeps people alive.

The best years of my life lie ahead—so long as I keep challenging myself. As with my welding, I will learn to fix things and also learn what cannot be fixed.

Having only a dozen harvests left forces me to ask how I can make the most of these remaining opportunities.

When Marcy asked me how many harvests I had left, she actually may have been talking about more mundane concerns than my philosophy of farming. She sees that I can't lift as much as I used to, muscles ache, joints sometimes fail. I squint when I study the horizon. In the winter, I get chilled easier and wear more clothes. In the summer, I wear long sleeves and big hats to protect myself from the sun. My body takes longer to recover from little injuries. Sometimes—and here's the scariest part—I'm not sure how I was injured in the first place, so I don't know how to avoid it next time. I can't fix things with brute force anymore. I have to think my way out of problems and search for solutions. Amazingly, I'm finding smarter ways to get things done, and also learning to ignore what can't be done. Older and wiser, I'm forced to take a slower path.

Yet these are minor issues. I never sensed my own mortality more than the moment I had to take away keys from Dad.

After relearning how to drive the tractor, Dad resumed work, disking, plowing, furrowing, mowing. After I had adapted our Massey Ferguson 255 to accommodate his disability, it became his favorite tractor. He had some trouble in the orchards, where we have to dodge and avoid low branches, but in the vineyards he could speed down row after row, churning with energy and a sense of accomplishment.

For months we had few incidents. No major accidents, just some stakes yanked out by a wandering disc or a few vines that he struck and ripped out. We could tolerate that minor damage (and we rationalized it by saying that those vines were so old that they'd probably wanted to be put out of their misery).

Then it came time for cane cutting. In the middle of the summer, the grapevine canes grow too long and hang from their trellis wires. If they're allowed to grow untrimmed, a disc or plow can hook and grab hold of the branch, pulling it off—along with the grapes. So we cut these canes a few feet above the ground, clearing a safe path for our tractors. By pruning off the excess growth, we also ensure that more of the energy that the plant is making goes to the grapes—not to leafy growth, or canes, or more vines.

The machine we employ to cut the canes has a rotary head and a mounted hydraulic motor. Connected to the motor is a flat cutting blade that whirls at hundreds of RPMs, slicing and dicing any hanging canes in its way. The cane cutter looks like two lawn mowers mounted on each side of the tractor, directly in the path of low-hanging canes.

The work can be violent: wood shatters and the spinning blades create a dizzying hum that is punctuated by the snapping of canes. The danger is to the vines, not the driver, since we have a mid-mount model, with the cutters to each side and in front of the driver, who sits safely out of the way.

Nonetheless, for me, cane cutting always carries a dreadful image. Years ago, when a neighboring farmer was working the vineyard near his house, his aging eighty-year-old mother, who had displayed numerous signs of dementia for years, wandered into the same vineyard. Not knowing she was there, he struck her with the cane cutter, which sliced into her legs. She quickly bled to death. My emotions churn with thoughts of all that farmer must have felt.

One day, about five years after Dad's first stroke, Marcy and I noticed that he was swerving badly while driving the cane cutter up and down a few rows. His erratic driving reminded me of the tracks from his drive that day to the shed while a clot was choking off the blood from parts of his brain. Now, watching him, we worried that he had developed another problem.

Dad's driving had actually become dangerous for him and the vineyard. The sharp cane cutter blade spun and wedged itself into a vine trunk before working free, then it sliced off good canes that were heavy with grapes. At the end of one row, Dad climbed off the tractor to untangle a matted jumble of young vine canes from the cutter but forgot to shut off the motor. The whirling blade spun inches from his work gloves; he did not realize the danger lurking below his fingertips, like a novice trying to clear a clump from a lawn mower.

I raced up to Dad and screamed at him to stop, but he finished clearing the brush and climbed back onto the tractor. He was sweating, his face glistened, and he appeared to be breathing hard.

He looked at me blankly.

I yelled: "You have to stop. Didn't you know the tractor was still running?"

He ignored me. I was not sure he could hear or was pretending he could not hear over the rumbling tractor engine.

"Stop, Dad!" I repeated.

For a moment he looked confused, puzzled by my frantic actions, but then he seemed to realize his mistake.

"Stop. Get off the tractor!"

His face tightened and he growled, his mouth open, his voice wanting to form words. Then he blurted what sounded like, "Damn! Shit!" and shook his head. Waving at me to go away, he jammed the gearshift into first and, with a jolt, careered down the vine row. I stood at the end of the row, watching him drive away. I could not stop him. For a moment I thought of running to my truck and blocking the other end of the vine row, forcing him to stop. But that wouldn't have been safe for either of us. Marcy caught up to me and asked what happened. I couldn't say.

That evening, after Dad had worked for an extra hour and washed up at the back door sink, I talked with him. He was calmer but looked very tired. Weary. He did not make eye contact.

I told him that he could no longer do specific jobs, especially cutting canes, because he could not work safely. He should not do certain types of tractor work. "It's too dangerous," I explained. And I took away the keys.

He frowned, then nodded. From that moment on, I had to limit his work. He could still drive the tractor, but first he had to get my approval. I felt lousy.

"Hope is the last to die" is said of people struggling against the odds, bravely confronting challenges, striving to overcome barriers. I feared I was removing Dad's last hope of ever feeling whole.

Learning what you can't do may be one of life's hardest lessons. One day my children or Marcy will have to tell me similar bad news. My best hope is that I'll already know it before we have that conversation.

If I'm lucky, I can approach these final harvests with a feeling of contentment, satisfaction. I try to keep this in mind: work is not solely about making money. I have measured success in rediscovering a perfect peach, in restoring it and its legacy to a new generation, in recovering organic traditions of cultivation, and in helping my father recultivate wisdom that he held in his body and mind, to recover his sense of self and purpose as I defined my own.

On the farm, much of my work is no longer about "my peaches." I find joy in growing things, contributing flavor to the world. I believe my good works will be rewarded. So, in return, I'm willing to give something of myself. I teach what I know and see that it can change the world, not with a vast project requiring huge amounts of resources and money. Instead, I simply focus on making things a little better than they were before.

This is how I want to be remembered.

When my grandparents were farmworkers, I don't think they had the luxury to project how many harvests they had left. They relied on themselves and worked to leave behind something better, no matter how limited a future they envisioned. Even as the relocation centers were finally closed after four years of holding Japanese Americans—citizens—captive, even as they made arrangements to return home to the West Coast, before leaving, many families swept out their barracks one final time.

When we recognize our mortality, our work carries new meaning. With a finite amount of time left, we see we have to act now, not later. Our lives are no longer about a personal definition of success but about creating significance.

I hope my final harvest is still years away. I'm happy still to be searching for the perfect peach as I count down these harvests. I'm still trying to figure out how to grow things, tell a great story, make a little money, and be a good person. For now, I like to cheat a little with my calculations and believe there are still thirty more harvests in me. That's a lot of time to practice doing good.

Chapter Twenty-five

COMING HOME

The Other California

When Dad's stroke hit, he was transported to another land. There he had to live in a new world of limits, where he would now and forever be defined by others.

We did not know that the greatest struggle would not be to recover more of his physical abilities, but to redefine his sense of self and success. An aunt once described my father as the strongest seventy-year-old man she knew. His strength would be tested.

As my daughter, Nikiko, went off to the University of California, Berkeley, I wondered how she would define herself and begin to redefine herself. When I was at Berkeley, I was embarrassed to say that I had grown up on a farm and that I came from the Central Valley. One of the reasons I chose to go to there was because I believed it was the one campus my parents would not come to visit. I was right. My mother spent fifteen minutes on campus as I unloaded my stuff for the dorms as a freshman and, four years later, came for graduation, which lasted a total of an hour and a half. Dad never came. We always had the raisin harvest in the fall, and during my graduation, the peach season was early and he could not get away.

He apologized, and I completely understood. Then he silently shook my hand.

In San Francisco, farmers were called "hicks" and "hayseeds" and places like our valley considered "backward" and "provincial," so I suggested that Nikiko simply say that she was from "the other California."

The rest of the state and world often define us by what we are not. The Central Valley is not Southern California, with its palm-tree-lined streets, balmy weather, big cities and sprawl, movie stars, and freeways. We're not Northern California, either, with its invigorating cool breezes, art, culture, and haute cuisine. We're part of the state that is often invisible, lost between north and south, part of an inland desert that doesn't seem to belong. The economic boom of Silicon Valley and Hollywood evaded us, but our valley is a good place to raise a family as well as crops.

In some ways, we have allowed others to define our identity. As outsiders moved in, amazed at the cheap prices of land and housing, we welcomed them and let them tear up our farms to make way for bedroom communities for Bay Area workers. They have tried to change us and remake the other California into a region that is indistinct and secluded, a place to pass through while on the way somewhere else.

After the stroke, Dad slowly became invisible, although I don't believe the family tried to conceal him. He retreated to his fields, where he felt comfortable. Other seniors, too, are hidden in rural areas or tucked away in small towns and cities, left behind in areas—in other Californias—that younger generations escape.

This is the danger for the other Californias: we don't trust our voices, so we hide our stories, and they are forgotten. We deny the value of our own cultures and become invisible ourselves. Without stories we are empty. Our stories tell the world who we are and what we hope to be. It's easy to neglect who we are when we become overwhelmed by what we are not.

Yet our valley teems with diversity. The length of Central Valley, from Bakersfield to Chico, is as ethnically and economically diverse as a drive from San Diego to Eureka. Should the big earthquake subtract the California coast and make our valley farmland into coastal property, our diversity will no longer be invisible. Imagine Chico as a reincarnated Mendocino, with Sacramento and Stockton becoming San Francisco and Bakersfield our "So-Cal." Then Fresno could be Monterey. And Del Rey becomes the new Carmel, with our farm part of the 17-Mile Drive.

Okay, I accept being from the other California. We in the other California may not shine as brightly or bloom as boldly as other parts of the state, but I like to think of us as a home for wildflowers of botanical and human varieties. We have a physical and geographic link to the land—regional in orientation, specific to a place. A big-city bias is that wildflowers are weeds, and others can make that mistake, too.

Dad himself made that mistake. One spring, Marcy and I planted thousands of wildflower seeds, sowing them in the vineyard, hoping they would find a home in our fields and keep out really undesirable weeds that compete with the vines for sun and nourishment. Soon after, we left for a weekend trip and asked Dad to watch the house. Having trained himself to purge the farm of all weeds, and thinking he was helping us by cleaning up our yard and fields, he dug out the strange plants.

When we got back, Marcy was angry and wanted to march over to the folks' house and talk with Dad. I restrained her and volunteered to tell him, myself. Later, when I explained to him that we wanted the wildflowers, I realized how hard it is to retrain our beliefs, to convince our brains to think differently. To Dad, those plants were weeds, and one of his main jobs as a farmer was to eliminate them. To him, they were in the wrong places, whatever they were, and, as he pointed out, "How can they be wildflowers if you planted them?" The conversation was much harder than I expected, and I sensed that Dad thought his work was no longer valued. He slipped back into the other California and stopped weeding near our home.

But wildflowers are hardy. They adjust to changing conditions, demand little maintenance, and often survive in niches under a broad range of conditions. And they did reemerge around our land.

Wildflower seeds are spread by the wind and can lie quiet and dormant for years where they fall, waiting to sprout with the proper conditions. They have learned the power in mobility. They, like my father, accept, adapt, and adopt.

My daughter, Nikiko, is also a wildflower. Like her great-grandparents, immigrating from one culture to another, she is carving a place for herself in an alien world. Like her grandfather, she is at home with farming. Part of the natural beauty of a place that still has a sense of the wild, Nikiko is more country than big city. She embodies the gift of the other California.

Truth Telling

A Japanese proverb says, "The crooked nail gets hammered down." Dad was one of those nails, returning to the farm, adjusting to the life of farming, pounded back by family, hammered by a country. As a farmer, I have both conformed to the valley and its people and worked to add something new. I've also tried to stand out in an industry that seeks uniformity. Although I strove to be different, I now realize I may be bent, like a crooked nail, and that I am getting pounded back into place.

A "good-enough" mentality thrives in our valley. Life is comfortable here, a good place to raise a family and be happy. Okay is fine for most people; things remain good enough because people rarely ask for more.

Good enough means things aren't that bad, which then implies that things must be good. As if being at the fiftieth percentile means you're better than others, at least half the others. And what's wrong with that?

A few years ago, an "outsider" superintendent arrived at a local school and questioned the district's "average" test scores. Teachers and parents responded: *Scores were at the fiftieth percentile, recently raised by five points!* The superintendent was eventually run out of town.

After Dad's stroke, we wanted to comfort him, accept his injury. Be patient. Be accommodating. Yet his recovery seemed to progress the best when he was challenged.

I didn't want a damaged father, so I sought to restore the old father, the working farmer. Dad shared my desire, as he was happiest when he was working. We were going to "beat this stroke," "take charge," "become survivors, not victims."

Seven years later, Dad had another major stroke, but even though we all again worked with therapists, Dad knew he could no longer work. He was not in immense pain, and he could still function, very slowly. He began to spend more and more time in his wheelchair. He enjoyed sitting outside in the sun rather than walking in the fields. He lost himself in a world with limits. He seemed comfortable.

I ordered a wheelchair ramp for the back door. At first Mom didn't like it—a sign of surrender. Eventually it, too, became part of this new world.

In our valley, we create communities of the comfortable, without the tension found in big cities. I'm not sure if we're blind to realities or if we do a great job of designing communities to avoid seeing inequalities. Freeways function as convenient, modern-day blinders when thousands drive past poverty and bad neighborhoods and are insulated from "those people" with problems. When I take the train, however, I pass the backyards of valley towns where reality can't be hidden. It's like touring another world, an uncomfortable world.

In the valley, a suburban mentality seems to dominate. People want neighborhoods that look more or less the same because sameness equates to contentment and a security in numbers. We're all generally happy (or all equally unhappy), with an emphasis on "all." Neighbors worry about sports, the price of gas, the next movie release, and the politics of saying "Happy Holidays" instead of "Merry Christmas." We seem to lack a focus on fundamental local issues and can't tackle the big ones, accepting a 30 percent high school dropout rate and tolerating rampant poverty that labels us as the new Appalachia.

Lurking beneath the benign "good-enough" thinking may be something more sinister: an intolerance of difference.

As I farm, my advocacy of difference may have morphed into a passive tolerance. Pounded back into place by the farm community, I sometimes allow others to define who I am instead of continuing to forge that definition by my own standards. If Nikiko returns, she will be challenged to label herself here, too.

There is a radical streak in our family. Dad had an army story about his basic training. Once, Dad did not salute an officer. He claims he didn't see him, but the officer had driven past in a jeep and backed up when he didn't see Dad's salute, confronting him.

Dad said, "I didn't see you, sir," and when questioned, he refused to apologize, sticking to his original story. Dad was punished with KP (kitchen police) duty and spent the next few weeks peeling potatoes. I'm not sure that Dad really did not see that officer. We are often tested in surprising ways and our actions become the clearest response.

In our valley, we may not be intolerant of change, but we often simply ignore difference. People remain invisible like ghosts dotting the landscape: the poor, those who struggle in our educational system, non-English speakers, undocumented workers, laborers at minimum-wage jobs. We tolerate them with an indifference that equals complacency. It all fits a good-enough rhythm: excellence is rarely sought. We ask why instead of why not. Greatness is reserved for other places. We accept lower standards, concede defeat. There is no "there" here.

Do we even want a "there"? Life is much simpler when you only believe in good enough. A "don't worry, be happy" mentality is much less stressful. I sleep better at night, I'm not as angry when I don't argue. I may live longer with acceptance instead of dying young fighting something unwinnable. Yet we can make good enough better by taking care of what we have—a slower culture, built on a regional perspective, with a strong working-class mentality, diverse and mixed ethnically. Then add a will to be great and we begin to grow up. But first we need to go beyond good enough.

While in the relocation camps during 1943, questions about loyalty were raised and all Japanese Americans over the age of seventeen were required to answer a questionnaire. Two specific questions challenged families. Question 27 asked: "Are you willing to serve in the armed services of the United States on combat duty, wherever ordered?" Question 28 asked: "Will you swear unqualified allegiance to the United States of America and faithfully defend the United States from any and all attack by foreign or domestic forces, and forswear any form of allegiance to the Japanese emperor or any other foreign government, power, or organization?"

Answers were complex, not necessarily a simple yes and no. Men were asked to serve in the armed services while their families were locked up in desert prisons. Immigrants from Japan were asked to denounce their native lands while their adopted country imprisoned them.

The majority answered "yes-yes." Some rebelled at having their loyalty as legal American residents or citizens questioned. Young men challenged the authorities and protested their induction into the armed forces, becoming "draft resisters of conscience." They demanded that their rights be restored. The Japanese-American community labeled them as "no-no boys."

My father and all his brothers answered "yes-yes." They were drafted and served in the army. One uncle became a translator of Japanese and fought in the Pacific.

The issue divided the community, even after the war. Growing up, every once in a while I'd hear reference to a farmer, people called him a "no-no boy" with negative connotations. The issue remained painful for some, even forty years later. In the 1990s when groups sought to recognize these "no-no boys" for their strength to take a stand of conscience and resist the draft, a huge argument and debate unfolded. Old wounds remained. Telling the truth had no simple answers.

I hope that Nikiko will come home and become a truth teller, someone who promotes action and change. It is a difficult path. Sometimes it's hard to be honest—in this valley and elsewhere. Telling the truth can create distrust. We live in a culture of affirmation; many listen only to those who agree with them. The right and left are polarized and listen to their own political pundits in the media. Rarely do they listen to each other. To be analytical of one's own position and side is often criticized and condemned. We live within a culture of separation, easier to categorize one another than try to understand one another. Many find black-and-white divisions simpler, easier to accept. Grays are disturbing and require effort to decipher.

Having lived here now for decades, I have caught myself worrying about the personality clashes that will occur if I ask the hard questions, and I have begun to accept the plight of the invisible poor. That's why I hope that my daughter, a new generation, will come home. We need young voices willing to talk instead of confront, to reflect and decide to act and take responsibility, to speak aloud and to speak with their actions. Truth telling is often a slow process; it requires you to stay put for a while.

During World War II, some good neighbors of the interned Japanese Americans took care of their property and farms. Some shared the profits of a revitalized wartime economy. (The price of raisins for the decade of the Great Depression averaged $55 a ton. During the war years, the price rocketed up to $192 a ton.) They were called "Jap lovers." Neighbors glared at neighbors, whispers and rumors persisted behind their backs; others openly challenged their helping and abetting the enemy.

These acts of kindness were often unrecognized and lost behind the hysteria of war. One good neighbor said, "It was the right thing to do." He also, upon request from his interned Japanese-American neighbor, helped deliver some furniture and belongings to the displaced family. As he drove in the middle of the Arizona desert toward Gila River Relocation Center, he kept thinking, *What a godforsaken place for America to lock up these people. Why?* He never forgot the drive. He realized he was doing the right thing despite the "back talk" back home.

Now that I'm part of the problematic status quo, the things my daughter will want to fight for might be different from what I want to fight for, but as my father accepted me and my new ideas, I will try to accept her and her ideas. Our farm has changed in the thirty-two years since my return. I had a long learning curve, time to transition to organic methods, replant orchards, relearn to farm the old way. I recovered old stories, created new ones. My daughter will need to learn at her pace, too, old stories and new.

Nature and family have long timelines. They have taught me well. It will take time for Nikiko to lose herself in these fields. Then, when I am no longer here, she will take care of the land as she too becomes the land.

An old advertisement about agriculture reads, "One generation farmed with their backs. The next farmed with equipment. The future will farm with their heads."

It reminds me of a story that a nisei (second-generation) Japanese-American farmer once told me. The family had lived the immigrant's success story, arriving with dreams, making opportunities, and achieving success through hard work. The farmer explained: "You know how the first generation immigrants were about work. You're only happy and healthy if you're working." He paused and grinned. "My folks worried so much about me growing up the right way, I swear they planted weeds to make sure I always had enough work to keep me busy and out of trouble."

I suppose you could say that Dad and I have planted lots of weeds for our successor. We also created an identity and character that we care about. Dad had his story; I've tried to establish my own. Should my daughter come home, she, too, will leave a mark. Perhaps the best I can do is make sure I don't stand in the way of her story.

We can romance the next generation by creating memories and trust. Memories of great tastes from our family harvests: eating the first ripe peach of the year and smacking our lips. Trust in the stewardship we practice: the belief that we can make a difference, even on the small scale of an eighty-acre organic farm.

Chapter Twenty-six

NAMES WE WEAR

WHILE CLEANING UP after a long day's work, I found, tucked high on a shelf in Dad's barn, an old tin coffee can in which Dad had saved dozens of rubber hand stamps, with the names of the various fruit varieties we once grew on the farm. The stamps' wooden handles were worn smooth from use over the years. When we used them, the rubber lettering gradually collected sawdust and dirt and periodically had to be scraped out with a nail. Several stamps named varieties that we had pulled out and no longer grew, but many others are old friends we continue to maintain.

Only one stamp had the Masumoto name. We rarely used it, reserving it for a few special orders and circumstances. The rest of the time, the thousands and thousands of boxes we packed over decades carried only the name of the fruit. We were invisible.

J. H. Hale
Stanwick
Elberta—the queen of peaches, buttery
sweet with a succulent yellow flesh

Few people grow these old peach and nectarine varieties anymore. They aren't as big or brightly colored as commercial brands, nor are they as long-lasting as newer hybrids, which can stay rock hard for weeks in cold storage after harvest, satisfying fruit brokers and produce managers, although rarely satisfying customers' taste buds. Oh, were these old peaches delicious! Elberta, in particular, is a beautiful peach with a sweet, buttery flavor and smooth consistency. It nestles in your palm, its lovely soft peach fuzz as comforting as a beloved dog's velvety ears. Juicy, fragrant, the queen of peaches, famous even in the nineteenth century as good eating and good for canning. Abandoned Gold Rush–era mines throughout the West carry remnants of Elberta peach cans, once an edible gold, shipped from the East Coast, California fields were quickly planted in the late 1800s to supply a growing West Coast population.

Hale, Stanwick—these were names from a simpler time when we knew all the peaches by name because there were only a few varieties. Now new varieties are introduced annually, some bred to bear earlier, some later, others specifically to increase shelf life and remain firm in cold storage.

There are so many new varieties that fruits today are rarely sold by name. Peaches are now simply peaches. They have lost their individual identities in a generic marketplace.

Even though these heirlooms have gone from most of the valley's other fields, these old fruit hand stamps memorialize their past.

Forty-niner
Red Top
Early Sun Grand
Sun Crest—one of the last truly juicy peaches,
exceptional flavor, a "kitchen sink" peach because the
juices trickle down your cheeks and dangle on your chin

These hand stamps connect me with my history. As a kid, every summer, I lived with these fruits, pressing their names onto wooden boxes. My fingers wore perpetual purple ink stains, and one summer I spent weeks with "Forty-niner"—the name of a freestone peach—stamped on my arm like a farm boy's tattoo.

Of course, some of these lost varieties had flaws. Some were naturally small or prone to having split pits when they grew too fast during a spring with abnormally warm temperatures. Others were overly sensitive to weather swings—a cool spring night made them a funny shape; a heat wave prior to harvest would promote a soft, easily bruised tip, which makes a peach spoil faster. But I can safely say that virtually every old variety tastes better than the varieties that are now most common in big supermarkets. And, in spite of these newer hybrids' long shelf life, they often deteriorate in texture, becoming mealy, mothy, and mungy on the tongue, unpleasant. Sometimes this is due to their having been stored improperly, but most often it's because they were picked too green and weren't yet mature. Even a wonderful heirloom peach will not taste good if picked too early. A green piece of fruit will never mature.

These old stamps set off echoes of memories of our family farm through the years and remind me why I love their taste, hoping my fruits create similar moments of joy for others.

Alamar
Nectar
Le Grand—large nectarine with yellow flesh
and savory flavor that's both tangy and sweet,
considered the grandfather of most nectarines

While I was growing up, our family did not have our own fruit label, a rectangular paper attached to the end of a fruit box identifying the farmer and the farm. A label marries the produce with the producer. We Masumotos did not brand our fruits by attaching our name to our peaches or nectarines.

Part of the reason had to do with marketing. For decades we sold our fruits to Sunnyside Packing Company, a Japanese-American owned-and-operated fruit distribution brokerage house. Dozens of other Japanese-American family farms participated in this arrangement, pooling our boxes of peaches to sell to buyers. The sales and shipping transactions were managed by Sunnyside for a 10 percent commission, and we packed our fruits into the Sunnyside box, which had a label imprinted with the word TRUWAY in red and white lettering.

Dad liked having this relationship, claiming: "I did my best work in the fields, so let someone else do the selling." Also, after relocation, few returning internees had resources to set up marketing relationships in addition to farming. Pooling their produce made sense. Sunnyside made a good partner. Dad and other farmers survived by employing their strengths, working with what they had and not what they didn't have. Also, it was hard to be Japanese American following World War II. Having your own name on a box of fruit could hurt sales, as if the peaches would have tasted different from a farmer of Japanese descent.

Merril Gem
John Rivers
Gold Dust—yellow-fleshed freestone with blushed golden skin, superb, old-fashioned peach flavor

When I read aloud these names, I also think of our neighbor farmers who have passed on: Kamm Oliver and Kei Hiyama. I grew up with these older men, wanting to believe we'd be neighbors forever. With their deaths their sons became our neighbors, a welcome continuity of generations of farmers, so rare today, when the history of a farm can be counted in a couple of years, rather than in multiple generations. The language of succession has changed. Taking over a family farm meant one thing for my grandparents and parents, another thing for me, and will likely be very different for my children.

We still use two of the original stamps for our Sun Crest peaches and Le Grand nectarines. These stamps honor Dad and his history on our farm. They are names we wear.

Regina
Flavortop
Babcock—one of the original white-flesh peaches, low in acid and sweet as honey

We farm memories into our fruits: eating a fresh Babcock peach or Le Grand nectarine becomes a moment of epiphany. If we've done our work correctly, it's no longer about our fruits but rather the creation of a personalized story of flavor, a spirit of perfection that goes beyond our farm's boundaries. They instill a hunger for memory—not nostalgia and longing for a past that can never again be, but memory that's alive with a passion for excellence.

I think of our peaches as art and want them to tell stories worth remembering. Great fruits work with a memory economy—consumers driven by desire anchored in the experience of flavor. Mass-produced fruit is designed to excite only the visual sense, but biting into a great fruit becomes a journey into taste, texture, and aroma. We artisan farmers strive to grow personalized produce, a signature that travels along with each piece of our work.

A great peach focuses us in the present moment and also transports us to someplace else: the memory of a tree in a grandpa's backyard, of mothers and daughters in summer kitchens canning peaches or making jam, of summer visits to a farm where we lost our peach virginity and truly tasted flavor for the first time. The peach taste tells you of its own time and place, the feel of the warm sun on its leaves, the energy of its veins and flesh as it draws its nourishment and water up through stem and root, its love of minerals and elements from deep underground, mined by rootlets and transported cell by cell into the perfect balance of sweet and acid. It's the fruit of the tree of knowledge of good and better. These stories join our meals, wonderful foods providing a social connection to places and people.

With stories, we never eat alone.

Flavor Crest
Sparkle
Baby Crawford—juicy texture with a classic peach flavor, descendant from the Crawford family of peaches

Many people—an entire generation—have grown up without ever having tasted a great peach or nectarine. Instead, their knowledge of fruits is based on a peach-flavored jelly bean or fruit roll-up. Super-sugar sweetness all too often becomes their criterion for taste. Without a memory of authentic taste, consumers think only in terms of cheap prices, and peaches then become a commodity. Who's going to demand a peach that they've never had? Gone are the words that help commit experience to memory; we lack a language of taste and meaning. In 1984, George Orwell foresaw a state-mandated language, Newspeak, from which words for love and other emotions not controllable by the government had been expunged. This Newspeak had a reduced vocabulary and grammar that diminished the range of thought and experience. Today the loss of a diversity of fruit robs us of our sensory language, our elemental heritage and connection to the good earth. And when foods lack a heritage, a story, certainly the farmer's voice and role in its cultivation will also be lost or dismissed.

We acquire memory by experience. Farming is about passing on what we know and what we create—food, knowledge, legacy, interconnection. Dad carried an indigenous knowledge gleaned from decades working the same piece of land. He knew how to respond to a change in weather conditions—which fields will dry out rapidly versus which have pockets of clay that retain water. He created a type of native competency for our farm world, a sense of knowing. Knowledge lives in the flavor of a peach or nectarine. By saving old fruit stamps, we save an old variety from total loss and homelessness. But without the memory of an experience, you have no sense of what you have lost—no sense experience at all, not sight, smell, taste, or touch. To many, the Sun Crest peach or the Le Grand nectarine are invisible—secrets.

The world doesn't need any more secrets.

June Crest
Red Haven
Rose Diamond—a newer nectarine with a surprisingly rich candylike sweetness

After I returned to the farm and we began to grow selective fruit varieties for organic markets, I wanted to differentiate ourselves from other businesses by finally creating our own fruit label.

I began with the goal of making the invisible visible.

I started with our name, then added *Family,* to point to our multiple generations: MASUMOTO FAMILY FARM.

Mas, Marcy, Nikiko, and Korio, Jiichan, and Baachan were all included in that name.

I added a symbol of culture, a Japanese kanji character 人—*hito*—which translates into "people." Another farmer once explained how to write it to me, "You know *hito,* written in two strokes. A long one with the other holdin' it up."

With this label, we include the story of a family farm and forever attach our name to the fruits of our labor. We add ourselves to each box.

Now we have a public face. We have a good reputation, but we also have the threat of failure at each harvest. I feel privileged to take such a risk.

When I show the finished label to Dad, he grins. Mom takes a picture of it, even though soon we will have thousands of boxes stamped with our label.

Royal Haven
Late Le Grand
Rio Oso Gem—a peach with character, not pretty with pronounced sutures but with firm flesh and distinctive "orange" flavor

These old names of fruits sound wonderful, like poetry. They incite a hunger for experience and they transmit the language of another culture, one that we can rediscover and teach to others so that it is transmitted through the ages and lets that poetry become part of our personal history.

Chapter Twenty-seven

ABANDONING A VINEYARD

FARMING TEACHES ME that nothing is permanent. In nature, things should not stay the same. We are all mortal.

Old farms always had odd crops growing in spaces too narrow for normal use but too valuable to be wasted. A row of plum trees along the ditch bank. A persimmon tree or two at the end of a vine row where the tractor turned and could drive under the branches. Early-blooming fruit was planted next to rock walls that preserved heat.

Dad tried not to waste space on the farm. He planted trees within a few yards of the house and shed. We grew a few orange trees on one part of the farm, on ground too high to be watered adequately for trees or vines (otherwise he'd have had to leave that area fallow). A walnut tree grew over the septic tank where it was not safe to drive a tractor (and thus could not accommodate an extra row of grapevines). Walnut trees also grew by the side of the road—during harvest, we'd knock and shake walnuts from the branches, so that they'd fall to the ground and asphalt; then a small group of us workers would run out to sweep the harvest off the road to the side, quickly scouring the earth, filling buckets and buckets while dodging any cars or trucks that came rumbling down the road.

Farmers grew multiple crops, some only for their own personal use. Small harvests were often given away, since they were of limited economic value. But I remember the smell of warm persimmon cookies in the fall, walnuts in baked goods, and fresh oranges from our backyard tree, picked first thing in the morning, chilled from the night air. We made good use of space on the farm.

In 2006, a bulldozer arrived and parked in the avenue overnight near my folks' house. In the morning, the dull yellow machine would pull up fifteen acres of grapevines. Dad looks through the window of his house, studying the sleeping monster, and I remind him of why it's there. He nods, then shrugs and indicates I should make sure the doors and windows are shut to keep out the dust.

The machine will begin with our eighty-year-old vines. These aging vines will fall quickly, their roots grown shallow, receding with age, their canes and canopies weak, easily collected by the dozer's forks.

I'm destroying about eight thousand of these old creatures because of the collapse of raisin prices. From 2000 to 2004, it wasn't fun to grow grapes for raisins. In 1999 the price a farmer received for a ton of raisins was about $1,200. In 2000 it fell to under $500, and, for the next three years, it hovered about $500 to $600 per ton. The year 2002 was brutal, prices tumbling to under $400 a ton. It costs about $500 to $600 to grow a ton of raisins if you do most of the work yourself and are willing not to be paid until there are profits.

The pain of the surplus was shared by all grape growers, including wine and table (fresh market) grapes. Industry leaders proclaimed, "California is drowning in a flood of grape juice." During this time, more than seventy thousand acres of grapes were pulled out in California.

Capitalism calls this creative destruction, supposedly part of the changes necessary for the evolution of an industry and eventual transformation. Modern farming is geared toward productivity, the excess in grapes partially due to short-sightedness and a greedy race for profits. Supply greatly exceeded demand, resulting in lower prices and eventual demolition. Our small operation joins in this inventive exercise called obliteration. The bulldozer roars, vines fall, capitalism prevails.

The vineyard we will sacrifice is our oldest, and its production capacity had fallen in recent years, partly because of the time constraints I face in farming. I was burnt out and the vines were burnt out. These were the hardest fields to farm, their earth was poor, more sand than loam. Their irrigation water required lots of pressure—it had to be "pushed" to travel from one end of the row to the other. Also, these older vines need a jolt from a fast-acting fertilizer to jump-start more new growth, but with the low price of raisins, I cannot justify spending additional resources on them. Also the current organic fertility programs I use, with their slow-acting compost and natural additives, will work too slowly.

As in most small businesses, the owner-farmer is the last to be paid. Any profits have to come out of the last fields that we harvest. (A parallel might be a restaurant that needs to average fifty meals served nightly—profits only come with the fifty-first plate out of the kitchen.) Because these weaker vines were the last to sugar and mature, we harvested them at the end, but any hope of profit has faded this year as harvest crews raced through the rows, working fast because of the light crop. My spirits sank at the sight of the poor quality of the grapes in each bin.

It's tough to end a year with your worst effort. The final impression stays with you for an inordinate amount of time. (A professional football player whose team lost in the final playoff game because of a fumble said that, throughout the off-season, he couldn't help but repeat, "Damn," over and over. He felt bad for his kids—they began to think part of their names was "Damn.") I think of the wasted hours and hours spent in those fields, diligently replanting dozens of vines after the oldest ones had passed.

A month before the bulldozer arrived, Mom had asked why the vines were not pruned. I explained my plan of vine removal. A week later, she asked again, and then again, wondering if I were making a mistake, wanting to help by repeatedly asking. It only made it worse.

I had failed; the next generation is supposed to improve on the labor of the last, not expunge it. But I can no longer properly nor sufficiently weed, cultivate, and irrigate this vineyard.

These vines were planted in 1918, the year my grandmother emigrated to America. My grandparents may have worked in this vineyard during the 1920s, as it was then one of the few farms owned by Japanese Americans, the Hiraoka family, until they lost it during World War II. In 1953, my grandfather passed away while Dad was expanding this vineyard. Whenever I work this field, I think of the grandfather I never knew.

Rows 25 and 26 in this vineyard are the site of Dad's stroke in 1997. I had replanted the few vines his disc had ripped out on that day. They were now growing, bearing a small crop. I thought of asking the bulldozer to skip those vines, a memorial to Dad. But Dad was not dead. And why a memorial? So I could remember? I don't need a reminder.

"Each of us has to choose, in the course of his brief life, between endless striving and wise resignation, between the delights of disorder and those of stability . . . To choose between them, or to succeed, at last, in bringing them into accord," Marguerite Yourcenar wrote.

A series of small choices leads ultimately to the larger one of tearing out the old vineyards. For a decade, I have maintained this vineyard, while also having a family, writing, and paying more attention to our peaches than our grapes. This has taken a toll on the vines. The decision to write an extra hour a day means I'm not in the fields for that hour. I do not regret my choices, but the reality is this: I can't match Dad's old habits and work—and I don't want to. I tell myself it's okay to abandon the vineyard without fault. There's freedom in an admission of failure and limitations.

Ironically, the tipping point lies with a different kind of vine, a weed called a puncture vine. Sometimes called "goatheads" (because two thorny prongs angle upward like horns with a third pointing downward like the beard of an old goat), these weeds thrive in dry, uncultivated sections of a field, along roadsides and avenues, under fencerows and near walkways, growing close to the ground, unnoticed as they spread horizontally, stretching out their branches, sometimes forming a dense mat. One large plant, unchecked, will produce thousands of seeds (scientific publications refer to the seeds of the puncture vine as "fruits"—which gives them a much too benevolent designation).

The miserable seeds grow in a woody burr cluster that has numerous small, very sharp points, about one-fourth to one-half inch in length. These stickers attach to any surface and spread, thus ensuring survival of the species, and its spines will penetrate anything—tractor tires, bottoms of work boots, animal hooves and pads. Farm animals, especially dogs, will limp home, lifting a paw, begging for help.

Raisin growers panic when they discover puncture vines. The seedpods easily stick to a raisin and cannot be shaken free. No mechanical device can detach the barbed menace, so the millions of berries must be run over a screen and slowly hand-sorted and the burrs removed one by one—increasing expenditure and labor, decreasing profit. In a desperate struggle to clean their raisins, farmers have paid workers a bounty for each seedpod discovered during this reconditioning process. They then destroy the seedpods, preferably by burning.

A single puncture vine seedpod found in a raisin bin is justification for an inspector to "fail" the entire thousand pounds. For a few years, following seasons of poor peach prices in the 1980s, I worked as an inspector of raisins to supplement our income. I would fail a bin of raisins only when I found numerous puncture vine seeds—but it turned out that whenever there was one, there were almost invariably plenty more.

Because I farm organically and cannot use herbicides to purge my fields of puncture vines, I am especially vigilant. Whenever I spy a puncture vine, especially with the bright yellow flowers it sets just before seeding, I'll leap out of my truck or off my tractor to dig out the devils. Its seedpods will remain viable for years, so it's vital to prevent it from "fruiting."

In spite of my vigilance, however, I can't walk the fields like

Dad, shovel in hand, monitoring the land for the *abunai* (dangerous) weed. I don't have the patience. I don't have his acute vision. I don't have the time. So, every year I'll miss a small bed of puncture vines, which flourish with just a little water, lots of sunlight, and neglect. I've discovered large plants stretching ten to fifteen feet in diameter with thousands of seedpods. I'll spend hours trying to dig up the mother plant, carefully lifting it into a box, trying to avoid knocking off seeds. Inevitably some will become tangled and pop off; I'll then take off my gloves, searching for the pale brown seeds that blend into the hoary dirt. My bare fingers get pierced by the thorns, the only simple method to detect their location. By the end of the day, I'll return home with my hands bloody, spirit broken.

The little choices Dad made also led to larger ones. Each small shovelful of work on his daily farm walks led to larger and larger fields unencumbered by weeds. Dad's continued tenacity to keep shoveling year after year eventually brought me home to farm. A small shovelful of change leads to another generation returning to the farm. But my lack of shovelfuls result in puncture vines proliferating and fifteen acres of vines pulled out. I destroy Dad's decades of labor and part of his spirit that lives in the land and on the farm. I lose some of Dad.

As the bulldozer roars and rips the earth, tearing roots and scattering grapevines, I feel ashamed. I have no plans for these empty fields, no strategy to fill the barren land with young vines or trees or dreams, to renew the land, recover from the loss, reinvigorate the farm. I can accept that things are not perfect but this purging will be forever.

Together Dad and I watch the machine at work, growling as it turns and targets another row of grapevines. I can see disappointment in Dad's eyes, but I believe he understands my decision. We are silent.

Then, Dad swears. Even though he lost his voice after the stroke, he can cuss—"Shit!" "Damn!" "Shit!"—on rare occasions when he's angry or moody. Sometimes this happens when he gets frustrated, like when he drops something and can't lean over to pick it up or he spills a cup of water across the dining table. Once in a while, when he's having a bad day, a simple problem such as negotiating a doorway with his wheelchair triggers a chorus of swear words. Ironically, because Mom can't hear, she isn't troubled too much by these outbursts.

As we watch the dust from the bulldozer, Dad growls and shakes his head. I say: "Damn grapes." I may be imagining it, but Dad grins. "Damn grapes," I repeat.

According to neurologists, the language of swearing comes from a section of the brain not the center of everyday speech. Some believe swearing is a survival mechanism, stored in the primordial part of the brain, an embedded rage circuit that, when activated, could unnerve an attacker. Swearing for our protohominid ancestors evolved from early mammals screaming or screeching in warning, a distress cry coming from deep within, the brain alerting us to harm, giving us time to run. Similarly, Dad's swearing may be part of a fight-or-flight reaction to threatening or disturbing situations. Or he could be trying to tell me to pay attention.

Abandoning this vineyard may result in creative chaos as well as creative destruction. In abandoning the vines, I open the land and myself to new possibilities and connections. Out of the chaos of a ripped-up vineyard's once-orderly rows, something new may grow. I never had open land on our farm. Damn grapes.

One idea for the empty acres is planting my own fruit-tree nursery. I can experiment with different, even exotic varieties of fruits—not just peaches or nectarines or grapes, but other heirlooms. Many will probably fail to thrive, but how will I know unless I try? I will not worry about productivity and efficiency. This will not be an R & D site, but our family farm's R & R escape. Rare fruits. Experimental crops. The old and forgotten. New life for the obsolete. Damn grapes.

If I don't make money from these fields, I could turn them into a space for art. Open fields of Mas, a new definition of public space. David Smith, the metal sculptor, planted his art in the land and called it *The Fields of David Smith*. Throughout the year, his sculptures changed when blanketed with snow or framed by green growth. Instead of weak, unprofitable vines, I could add a different work of art each month—perhaps land art like Andy Goldsworthy's, using natural and found objects.

Farming itself is ephemeral art, changing with a season, a breeze, a sunrise—capturing moments in time. The pile of hardpan rocks that tumbles over with the first storm. The differences in the sandy loam earth after a spring rain or the baking heat of summer. A stack of dead peach tree branches that serves as nesting sites for birds, then crumbles with weathering, creating new dens for other wildlife who live closer to the earth. In the wake of the bulldozer that opens our farm, imagination thrives. Damn grapes.

I pat Dad on the back and tell him I have to run. He nods and waves.

I meet the bulldozer and yell to the driver: "You won't finish today, will you?"

He pulls up his goggles so that they rest on his dusty forehead. "Nope. Can't get it done."

"Tomorrow I have one more section to pull out, I'll mark it and direct you." I repeat, "Tomorrow."

He nods, pulls the goggles back down, and cranks up the diesel engine.

That evening I map out a new plan to remove two more vine rows. I want to create an avenue that can cut across a field. With the new path, I won't have to drive all the way around the block of vines and trees. It's possibly a waste of good vines, but now that I see open spaces I ask myself, *How often in life will I be able to create real shortcuts?* Damn grapes.

Chapter Twenty-eight

PRESERVATION

FARMERS WORK ALONE, in isolation, independently. Yet our work also is one of connection—with family, the environment, and ultimately with the public through what they eat.

As depicted on our Masumoto Family Farm label, farming means "people," *hito,* leaning on one another. The new family farmer has to lean on others, perhaps more than ever before.

As I did more of the farmwork after Dad's initial stroke, Dad began to make his own gourmet raisins. This was a new practice that Dad created, remarkable because, for all our years of farming together, we worked so hard during harvest that we barely got to enjoy our own fruits.

At the end of the harvest in late September, after the work crews had passed through the vineyards, Dad gleaned the fields for grape bunches that had been missed and overlooked. These were the sweetest grapes, having ripened a couple of extra weeks, lonely fruits that the grapevine had nourished with its last surge of nutrients. Often amber in color, they invited Dad to rescue them.

Our raisin grapes are mostly of the Thompson variety, a white, seedless grape of Turkish or Iranian origin, developed in California by viticulturist William Thompson in 1876. In Italy there's a great tradition of wine grapes being left on the vine to dry to make certain very concentrated wines. A wine called Amarone, for instance, is made from grapes that have been stored and allowed to dry almost into raisins, which are then crushed and fermented. In France, in cooler regions, some vineyards allow their grapes to stay on the vine to develop a fungal disease called botrytis, or "noble rot," which they use to create intense, viscous white dessert wines.

Drying grapes to make raisins is at least a four-thousand-year-old tradition, even mentioned in ancient Egyptian writings. Like the Mediterranean, our valley in California has an ideal climate for raisin grapes—lots of sun and mild winters. (The other major raisin producers are Greece, Turkey, Iran, Afghanistan, and Australia, but they're also produced in South America, China, South Africa, and Eastern Europe.)

The first vineyards planted in California were established by nineteenth-century Spanish missionaries, mostly for wine making, some of which are still producing today. But then farmers realized the value of raisins, which can be made sooner than wines, and they planted raisin grape vineyards.

For his gourmet raisins, Dad used old wooden two-by-three-foot trays—the traditional tool for drying raisins—but added paper trays on top. He spread the grapes on the trays so they could cure in the sun, filling the yard with dozens of these trays. He monitored them daily and, whenever there was potential for a rainstorm, stacked them and covered the top tray with an inverted empty one, protecting his final harvest. When the sun came out again, he'd unstack the trays so the grapes could continue their curing. In the past, this is how raisin grape farmers rescued a harvest, provided their farm was small enough and they had enough hands for the thousands of trays.

After three weeks, the raisins had dried, and Dad rolled them up in their paper trays and stored them in the shed. Every few weeks, throughout the fall, winter, and spring, he'd bring out another roll for cleaning. Especially on rainy days, he'd spread them out on the dining table and, one by one, remove the stems from the raisins. Mom then quickly rinsed the crop, blotted them dry with a towel, and stored them in bags or glass jars. At every breakfast, they served their own raisins with cereal or oatmeal. Dad had found a way to save the best for last and enjoy his harvest.

Mom has always served the best peaches, because she preserved them by freezing them. We did not grow up with a pantry full of canned fruits or rows of jars filled with jams and jellies; freezing peaches is easier and also preserves their nutrients.

During harvest I'd bring in peaches, slightly soft and gushy. Mom would then peel them by hand, gently rotating the golden sphere in her palm, guiding a paring knife through the yellow flesh. Then she'd slice them, lightly cook and store them, devoting an entire shelf in the freezer to plastic containers and bags with the bright slivers. She preserved the best heirloom varieties, one of the few times I witnessed a little selfish behavior from my folks. Why not have some of the best of the harvest for themselves?

Throughout the fall and winter, they'd eat the peaches for breakfast, sometimes alone, other times with cereal (and recently with Dad's gourmet raisins). Mom rationed the peaches throughout the year so they'd have enough for every breakfast until the next harvest. Her goal was to serve their own fruits every day of the year. It was a routine and part of Dad's recovery to always have comfort food from their own farm.

Mom, aunts, and neighbors also made Japanese preserves that we enjoyed at most meals. We ate *tsukemono,* cured and pickled fruits and vegetables that came from our garden or that neighboring Japanese farmers gave us. A favorite was *umeboshi,* pickled plums. We also ate a great wintertime treat called *ochazuke,* the perfect comfort food—warm white rice with hot tea poured over it and topped with our *tsukemono, umeboshi,* or dried or preserved seaweed. *Takuan,* pickled daikon (horseradish) was also served at most meals.

In winter we had a bucket of Chinese cabbage curing in the laundry room, resting in a salt brine, a wood lid pressed against the cabbage with a heavy chunk of hardpan on top to act as a weight. Doing the laundry made me hungry.

In the late fall, Baachan would hang a string of Japanese persimmons against the shed, drying them into *hoshigaki*—a sweet treat. In order for them to cure evenly, she had to massage them, gently squeezing the pulp inside the skins. Some years this continued into December—we joked it was her string of Christmas decorations dangling for all to see.

When I married Marcy, she brought her Midwestern German preserves into our household, jams and jellies, chutneys and mock mincemeats, from pickled relishes and krauts to tomatoes in sauce, frozen whole, canned, and juiced. She also made sauces from apples, cranberries, pears, and plums. Her family preserved almost anything; pickled watermelon rinds became a favorite of mine.

Until recently, preservation methods were vanishing. *Fresh* connoted healthy and *canned* had become a pejorative. The flavors of preservation—sour and bitter—fell out of favor. Once at an inner city school in Denver, I gave fifth-grade students a taste of our peaches via a special jam we make—a low-sugar recipe that still brings out the flavor of peaches. The students could not hide their initial reactions: puckered faces, pursed lips, eyes squinted. When I asked what they tasted, they said, "sour," "bitter," "nasty, like medicine." When I found out that their breakfasts at school consisted of Cocoa Puffs, Frosted Flakes, and Froot Loops, I realized that I'd purse my lips, too.

Lately, however, more and more families are discovering the joys of preserving their own foods from their own gardens and local markets. The high gas prices of 2008 turned many people into vegetable gardeners who loved the money they saved at the grocery as well as the gas they saved by not having to travel to the food store. And they discovered what all gardeners and farmers learn—when the crop comes in, it *really* comes in. You can't eat it all and you can't give it all away and you hate to see your zucchini, tomatoes, and eggplants go to waste and spoil. So canning has made a comeback. Newspapers and food magazines ran many more articles and recipes about preserving foods in 2008 than they had since the Great Depression.

The community-supported agriculture movement (CSA) has also helped keep local produce available and local farms viable. Members in a CSA farm pay a subscription price for about six months of produce that they start receiving every week as crops come in. Some CSA farms are organic and particularly like to grow heirloom varieties of vegetables.

Even so, these days people think of peaches more for how well they eat, rather than how they handle in baking or preserving. Decades ago, fruit brokers would ask Dad if our fruits canned well or if we had cooking peaches. They were looking for fruit for canneries and also to send to the Midwest where families gathered to can and preserve boxes of peaches in annual summer peach-o-ramas. Everyone had a job canning for winter. One of our older varieties, Forty-niners, worked well at the cannery. Strangers sometimes stopped at our farm, asking for Elbertas, recalling fond memories of baking, canning, and jamming. Many families passed down food traditions during these gatherings from one generation to another; family food memories that they created and preserved along with the peaches.

Even many of us farmers are unable to enjoy their own fruits, shipping off most of our own harvests. The urgency of a harvest can be overwhelming and the exhausting pace of the work can crush the joy we take in our perfect peaches or grapes or vegetables. On our farm, however, we are trying to revive traditions of appreciating our local harvest with an annual jam fest. We invite family and friends for an evening of peaches, work, and sweat. At the end of the evenings, participants take home jars of jam, lots of jam. We also dry our peaches into delicate slices to capture the flavor of summer harvest and celebrate it during the winter. Then we can experience that perfect peach that we ate in the summer again in the middle of winter, by preserving it to enjoy in a moment with less stress, more time for reflection. It is one way to put time in a bottle. And the food tastes better without summer stress.

Good food belongs at the table in all the seasons. I hope we can expand the definition of seasonality. You can still taste the best nectarines even in December if you've preserved them in a chutney. Rather than import fresh but rock-hard, tasteless strawberries in February, why not preserve nature's bounty so you can share it throughout the year. In the process, farms and farmers extend their seasons, broaden their harvests, and perhaps preserve their livelihoods.

During the off-season, I try to connect with consumers, finding time to visit, solicit responses, accept reactions. Working with a new economy of time—the luxury of peaches in January from dried peaches or preserves made in July—we can redefine "fresh." Preservation lengthens the life of food without sacrificing its tastes. Farmers can then work more directly with customers, and food consumption will determine the methods of food production. How people eat will determine how farmers farm. Social capital becomes part of a harvest. I don't want to be separated from the people who actually eat our fruits. As I seek new connections and seek to reframe traditions, my farming will participate in a food system where we learn to lean on one another.

Dad has taught me how to preserve. Preserve the farm. Preserve the land. Preserve tradition. Preserve flavor. Preserve memory. Preserve integrity. Preserve authenticity. Preserve culture. Preserve the past. Preserve trust. Preserve the art of farming. Preserve the art of food. Preserve the romance of work. Preserve the story.

Our farm now works with new partners—chefs and specialty fruit distributors. We open ourselves to the world with our farming story. We discover a new world of food where farmers are not the center but part of new partnerships. Sustainability is defined by economics, environmental responsibility, and fairness—as well as preservation.

Thirty or forty years ago, Dad chose the fruit varieties he would grow after conversations with neighbors, fruit brokers, at an industry meeting with researchers, at a community potluck dinner, at a funeral. At that time, new varieties were introduced only gradually, usually after extensive field tests. Farmers wanted to know how it did on a real farm before investing their land and time in a new fruit. This changed in the 1970s, when dozens of newly patented varieties were unveiled and marketing regulations started to set standards. The result has been a little like picking stocks—one out of five new hybrids will be great, the rest probably mediocre, and, if you're lucky, you won't plant the one that will fail completely. And I must admit that some new varieties, like Elegant Lady peaches and Rose Diamond nectarines, actually do taste good, with a flavor and aroma similar to some of the best heirlooms.

Gradually, I have expanded my own conversations, finding rare-fruit growers and gardeners who share my passion for flavor. We became friends often by sharing wood for grafting. Sometimes when we make the scion exchange (wood from one tree to be grafted onto another), I feel like a contraband dealer, arranging a private meeting, carefully cutting a small branch and quickly wrapping it in a damp cloth, storing it in a dark place, out of sunlight. Later, as I carefully unfold the cloth to prepare to graft it, I dream of the perfection that will stem from the staff of life in my hands.

Grafting is an almost mystical art. It seems magical to be able to take a small branch from one tree, cut a notch in the bark of another (the rootstock), and fuse the two together in one plant. They are then wrapped with string or tape to keep the bond sealed. If it works, the fruit of the tree from which the branch was cut will grow from that branch on the new tree. It's a fine art to learn how to consistently cut the scion wood smooth, position it correctly in the notch of the host tree. We line up the cambium layer—a thin layer between the wood and the bark that is the tree's circulatory system, transporting water and nutrients from the roots up to the leaves and vice versa—to ensure that it "takes" and grows. Many experts who do "topwork"—grafting—can convert one orchard to another with a 90 percent success rate.

Grafting, creating scions and new trees, is another ancient art of preservation, also at least four thousand years old, like drying grapes into raisins. On our farm, I work to fit the old traditions into our new world. People's lives change—people change. They can choose something that is better, when they have good choices. They don't change, however, if their choice is between bad and worse. Preserving our best fruits gives us choices. And it preserves our quest for the best.

We live and we farm believing in perfection: in a perfect peach, in a perfect pleasurable experience—like eating wonderful peach jam in January. Or Mom's freezer peaches in the spring. And Dad's gourmet raisins for breakfast all year round. We want everyone to have such perfect choices.

Chapter Twenty-nine

DAY IS DONE

The Ofuro / Japanese Bath

The *ofuro* is one of the traditions thousands of Japanese immigrants brought with them from the homeland, creating a personal bond in the simple act of cleansing, a communal act of family. Japanese bathed daily if possible, quite different from the rural "once a week on Saturday night" tradition that many American farmers practiced a hundred years ago.

Forty years ago, we had an old-style *ofuro* on the farm, modeled after those in Japan. Few immigrants could afford to import the authentic cast-iron baths from Japan, so my parents created an American version by fabricating a large metal box—about three feet wide, four feet long, and four feet deep—that held water and was heated by a fire beneath. Baachan's job was to make and tend the fire for the entire family. We began by washing thoroughly outside the tub, squatting to utilize a bowl to scoop out water to soap and rinse. Then we slipped into the hot liquid to soak. We took turns, the kids first. When we got out, Mom and Baachan got in. Dad was last because he usually came in late from work. We'd stoke the embers to reheat the water for him. Throughout the evening, the entire family shared the same soaking water.

My grandparents wanted to *ofuro* often because it reminded them of Japan, a connection with home, a remembrance of family. Closing their eyes, steam rising around, they returned to their homeland for a moment after a long day laboring in the fields, no longer aliens in a strange land. For Mom and Dad, the *ofuro* manifested their sense of place: part Japanese, part American.

Even though Baachan passed away more than a decade ago, I can visit with her whenever I bathe in an *ofuro*. In a junk pile, I found an old *ofuro* from my grandparents' era, cleaned it, and patched a slight leak. Our family could now reenact our American version of our Japanese tradition. Strong enough to last for decades, the galvanized sheet-metal box was riveted at the corners and felt very familiar, just the right size for small people; when we curled up, we could easily fit inside. The top edges were rolled and rounded, smooth and gentle to our bodies as we slid across the surface to slip into the simmering liquid.

I set up the *ofuro* outside, near the barn. To make the fire to heat the cold water for an *ofuro,* I used old redwood stakes and grapevine stumps. The fire burned brightly in the twilight, smoke curling around the metal tub, the flames licking it and dancing. I believe that the vine-wood smoke flavors the water. Summer is good for burning vine stumps and their gnarled and twisted black trunks, but winter calls for denser woods; peach and plum create hotter fires to keep off the chilling valley fog.

To the side of the *ofuro,* I've set up a similarly old raisin sweat box as a washing station. The sweat box is a long, flat box only a foot in depth but two to three feet wide and three to four feet long. It's a relic of the past when raisins were collected by hand after drying in the fields and stored for months before delivery. The wood helped even out the moisture, the raisins "sweating" to proper dryness. It's appropriate for our step back in time.

I bathe with Korio, so first we wash outside the tub. Scooping the water with a small wooden bucket made from pine, we can smell the scent of the mountains as the water cascades over our heads. It splashes on the sweat box, the sound of water dripping as we stand naked; a cool summer breeze tickles our backs in sudden contrast to the hot water. Again we rinse ourselves, shivering as the evening air descends on our skin with a gentle tingle.

We slip into the heated water, initially almost too hot, and find our footing on the wooden flooring. As our skin adjusts to the temperature, we squat, then sit, and the water rises across our chests, up to our chins. The world suddenly seems to slow down, the sunset's last light of day eases into night. Some drops from the tub splash onto the fire and hiss, a wisp of smoke wanders upward, a cleansing smell.

I tell Korio how Japanese immigrants would watch the sunset, knowing it would next descend on their native lands across an ocean. Baachan came to America to create a new homeland, to assimilate and become American, but also to respect traditions, like the *ofuro*. The first baths the immigrant families built were open-air, located away from the farmhouse, reducing the risk of an accidental fire. The tubs sat atop hardpan rocks, a fire beneath them. Later, a cement slab was poured so that splashes and soapy water could properly drain away from the fire. When I was young, almost every Japanese-American farm family had built a small wooden shack called a *furoba*, enough to keep out the weather and create some privacy (from curious children peeking through the cracks in the wood siding).

My mother likes to tell the story of when she had to make the fire—the job of the youngest child, because parents and older siblings worked long hours in the fields. Experienced fire builders knew how to make embers quickly in order to heat the water slowly and evenly, but Mom made a roaring blaze and the *furoba* caught fire. She never had fire duty again.

As a young child, I was always terrified that somehow the wooden raft would topple and I'd burn my feet. Since the water is heated directly by a fire, the bottom of the tub grows very hot, so a wooden raft keeps feet and bottoms from touching metal. Over the years, the water-soaked wood swells and slats become loose, so more nails, lots of nails, are pounded in to stabilize it. Even with all the metal nailed into the wood, I was too light to sink the raft into the water alone, so it became tradition that all of us kids took our *ofuro* together, the only way to combine enough weight for the wood to sink to the bottom so young bodies could soak. We played games, threatening to jump out and destroy the balance or pretending to be in an ocean and rocking to create waves, splashing liquid out of the *ofuro* and wasting hot water. I can still hear Baachan's voice as she tended the fire, scolding us kids with her low but shrill "ahhhh," imploring us to calm down but grinning as she shook her head.

Later, as a college exchange student living in the small Japanese village from which Baachan had emigrated, I took an *ofuro* in the same metal tub in which she had once bathed. Every evening her brother's family and I built a fire, washed and soaked, sharing the water. We relaxed, we told stories. I learned about family, farming rice, the history of the ancient farmhouse. Even Baachan's stoic brother, who took over the family rice farm, became conversational during the *ofuro*. This was a place for storytelling, for creating stories.

Now, each summer, I set up the *ofuro* and we take a family bath in perhaps one of the only working *ofuro*s left on a farm. We share the waters of history, a Japanese-American baptism. Perhaps we could make it chic by renaming it the "original California hot tub." Dad smiled when he saw me revive our old tradition and located an old, worn metal shovel with a broken handle, too weak for weeding but perfect for stoking the fire. We leave it leaning against the metal tub to use the next time.

This family tradition carries the meaning of culture, an almost forgotten act that was once a simple part of daily life.

After the *ofuro,* the best part remains: walking back to the farmhouse in the dark, body warm, cool air of the evening stroking my skin. No different from Baachan. No different from Dad. For a moment, all feels well.

Gone the Sun

I follow in Dad's footsteps, working long into the evening, as long as sunlight allows. I love summers, when I can work late until eight or even nine o'clock. Sometimes I work beyond the time when it's safe to do tractor work as I lose light while driving and have to start guessing where end posts are and vine rows begin. I trust tree branch outlines to guide my path. As I head home, the dusty avenues acquire a lighter, hoary hue, a white path to follow in contrast with the growing darkness.

I feel like the cowpoke riding home at the end of a hard day, the blue-collar laborer working overtime to complete a project. My clothes are laden with dust, my body aches. I'm fatter now and my painful joints carry the history of youthful abuse from old sports injuries and farm accidents. I go slower and yet feel fulfilled.

I started in the morning in fields of green and end the day with fading light over fields of gold. In these dark shadows lies life. Each workday helps define me. I am driven to accomplish something daily: disking weeds, opening furrows, checking irrigation water, monitoring pests, tying a falling limb, sawing a broken branch. I still seek perfection, not in outcomes but in effort. I trust myself and believe good can come from my labors: this is where I belong, I've earned the right to work a piece of land.

Evenings, I remember hearing Dad wash up, a routine of cleaning up before a late dinner. First, the noise of stomping work boots, next the sound of his hands patting down dusty work clothes. Then he'd remove his shirt and I could hear him whipping it against his pants, slapping at the embedded dirt, freeing more dust.

Our outdoor sink has no drain, so the water splashed onto a pile of small rocks then drained into a garden. I could hear the pauses when he stopped washing and drank, sometimes a long, slow drink of cool water. He ended in silence. We had no towels outside; in our dry heat we often drip-dried, an excuse to wait and suspend the day for a moment before coming inside.

I complete my workday with a ritual like Dad's that ends at the back-door sink. Removing my shirt, I rinse my hands then hesitate, debating if I want to wash up completely. I cannot simply wash my face, and I stick my arms and shoulders into the stream, too, watching the mud run off my skin. I tip my face under the faucet and feel the heat drain away with the water and dust, pausing before inserting my entire head. The water dribbles down my neck and back, and I shiver with the striking coolness, a reward for washing up.

Of course, I should have taken a shower or an *ofuro,* a soaking, a cleansing. But the family awaits inside for a very, very late dinner. So I toss my head back, and a trail of water whips behind me. I feel like a dog shaking itself. For a few minutes, I sit on a bench on the porch. In this arid heat, even at night, I will dry quickly.

Our house sits on the highest ground of the farm, not for the view but because this was the worst piece of land; a hidden hardpan layer sits underneath us, impenetrable to roots. That's the simple lesson these old farmhouses carry—on ground impossible to irrigate because of the height, on land that is worthless because water doesn't flow uphill and fruit can't grow on hardpan, that's where you build your home.

Yet from our porch, I can peer over the fields and feel like a king for a moment. A bright moon illuminates the beautiful, orderly fields. Memories fill the darkness and crickets trill.

Dad's stroke catapulted our family farm in different directions, challenging our quest for perfection, testing our work ethic, making us redefine our identities. I had to take over and find new ways to finish old tasks and reinvent old traditions that best address timeless tasks.

Succession implies a rebirth of identity and a renewal, but it also suggests the end. Dad slowly withdrew from the farm after his second major stroke, retreating into a mental fog where he does not seem to miss work and seems comfortable. I, too, will one day disappear from this land. Someone will take my place if it needs to be filled. Over time, my work will not be missed. In the end all we are left with are stories and memories that are acts of love.

After dinner with my family, I take a final walk of the day in the moonlight, the last duty before I rest. I navigate familiar paths I've traveled countless times, my memory of a pothole or mound guiding my pace. Ahead lies an irrigation pump I need to start in order to deliver water to a new orchard I planted with Nikiko.

We've added one more old peach variety—Gold Dust—to the farm. Another heirloom, a pedigree with the classic amber hue when ripe and a rich, deep flavor. For us, this peach carries added significance: when crossed with another heirloom, it created a wonderful hybrid that became a centerpiece of our farm story. Gold Dust is the parent of Sun Crest.

With this tradition of planting the old, we renew our commitment to the farm and to the future. We renew this promise out of love.

Acknowledgments

MY FAMILY LIVES within these stories. Marcy listens and responds accordingly as both a wife and life partner; I can't write these stories without her. Nikiko, my daughter, was always part of the farm and will find her own farm stories as she becomes a farmer and carries these stories forward. Parts of the story "Coming Home" first appeared as letters exchanged between Nikiko and myself during her first year of college. Korio, my son, keeps Jiichan smiling and laughing and shows the world another side of life. He helps remind me that life stories will always have a few surprises. My mom was and is a partner on the farm, and she cares for Dad just as he cared for the land: with emotion, absolute commitment, and a strength I can only hope to sustain. And to my father, who is the farm and will always be part of every harvest and of every story, I cannot farm nor write without you. I thank my family; all live in these stories.

Versions of some stories first appeared in the *Fresno Bee,* where I have been a columnist since 2002. I want to thank the *Fresno Bee,* especially Ray Steele, Charlie Waters, Betsy Lumbye, and Jim Boren.

A version of "Family Heirloom" was first published in the *New York Times Magazine* on August 13, 2006. Thanks to Amanda Hesser for her editing of that story.

I want to thank Malcolm Margolin and Heyday Books for granting permission to modify some stories that appeared in my two essay collections, *Letters to the Valley* and *Heirlooms.* Malcolm reminds me that stories do matter.

A special thanks to Elizabeth Wales, who is both an agent and friend and helped in the genesis of this book as it took many forms. Her persistence and caring nature gave life to these stories. Thanks also to Neal Swain, a great help as the book proposal took shape.

Acknowledgments

I am grateful for the support of Free Press, including Dominick Anfuso, Martha Levin, Suzanne Donahue, Carisa Hays, Kathryn Higuchi, Amy Ryan, and Jill Siegel. A special thanks to Donna Loffredo, editorial assistant, and Helen Chin, typist. Leslie Meredith, my editor, has become a new partner. She helps complete these stories with her unwavering support and sensitivity, along with insight. She would make a great farmer; I'd want her as a neighbor.

Finally, a thanks to those in the farming, food, and literary worlds. Dan Barber is a farmer's best friend, he inspires me, and I'm honored he wrote the foreword. Also thanks to Jesse Cool for our discussions about the seasonality of food.

I am grateful for conversations and support from others—a simple exchange often plants seeds that will grow into stories: Alice Waters, Poppy Tooker, Kristine Kidd, Craig McNamara, Rick Bayless, Daphne Dervin, Stuart Brioza, Nicole Krasinski, Paul Greenberg, Bill Fujimoto, and Jim Quay.

Organizations have also helped support both me and our family farm, including the Peters Rehabilitation Center at Community Regional Medical Center in Fresno, the International Association of Culinary Professionals, Slow Food, Sun-Maid Growers of California, Brandt Packing, Whole Foods, and, of course, Pacific Organic Produce.

Readers, neighbors, friends, foodies, and fellow farmers—I thank you for the exchanges that motivate and ground my stories. I hope this book speaks to many about our fathers, our farms, our foods, and the passion in our work.

About the Author

David Mas Masumoto is an organic peach and grape farmer who works with his wife, Marcy Masumoto, and their two children, Nikiko and Korio, on their eighty-acre farm just outside Del Rey, twenty miles south of Fresno, California. He has a bachelor's degree in sociology from the University of California, Berkeley, and a master's degree in community development from the University of California, Davis. He is a columnist for the *Fresno Bee,* has written for *USA Today* and the *Los Angeles Times,* and has been featured in the *Wall Street Journal,* the *Los Angeles Times, Time* magazine, and the *New York Times.* His farm has been featured in *Sunset, Country Living,* and *Glamour* magazines and on television as part of the *California Heartland* PBS series, as well as the nationally aired program *Ripe for Change.*

Masumoto has won numerous awards for his writing, including the James Clavell Japanese American National Literary Award in 1986. With *Epitaph for a Peach* he took the 1995 Julia Child Cookbook Award in the Literary Food Writing category and the San Francisco Review of Books Critics' Choice Award, 1995–96, and was a finalist for the 1996 James Beard Foundation Food Writing Award. He was the recipient of a Bread Loaf Writers' Conference fellowship in 1996. *Harvest Son* garnered a Commonwealth Club of California silver medal for the California Book Awards in 1998 and was a finalist for the Asian American Writers' Workshop prize in New York. In 2003, Masumoto received the University of California, Davis, Award of Distinction from the College of Agricultural and Environmental Sciences. He has been the keynote speaker at diverse conferences, including those of the International Association of Culinary Professionals, Culinary Institute of America, American Association of Museums, and many more. In 2007, he was a W.K. Kellogg Foundation Food and Society Policy Fellow.

Wisdom of the Last Farmer

Harvesting Legacies from the Land

David Mas Masumoto

Reading Group Guide
Author Q&A

ABOUT THIS GUIDE

The following reading group guide and author interview are intended to help you find interesting and rewarding approaches to your reading of *Wisdom of the Last Farmer*. We hope this enhances your enjoyment and appreciation of the book. For a complete listing of reading group guides from Simon & Schuster, visit BookClubReader.com.

INTRODUCTION

When David Mas Masumoto's father has a stroke in the fields of their organic peach farm in California, the reality of his father's mortality drives Masumoto to reevaluate the significance and meaning of farming in a fast-paced, modern world. As he nurses his father back to health, and becomes a teacher to the master who had once schooled him, he reclaims the practical and emotional wisdom that they and their ancestors had learned from working the land. Realizing that he himself needs to pass on a wealth of knowledge to the next generation, he writes this impassioned narrative about reconnecting to the land.

In *Wisdom of the Last Farmer,* Masumoto finds the natural connections between families and farming, fathers and children, booms and declines, and relates them to larger, more sweeping themes of life, death, and renewal.

DISCUSSION QUESTIONS

1. Growing up as the third generation in this country, David Mas Masumoto learns to embrace Japanese proverbs such as Fall Down Seven Times, Get Up Eight; The Crooked Nail Gets Hammered Down; and It Can't Be Helped. How do you think these perceptions influence his life and philosophies of farming? Can you relate these proverbs to your own life?

2. Masumoto's father's stroke occurs at the very beginning of the book. How does this affect your reading of the story, knowing that his father has suffered this trauma? How does this alter Masumoto's reflections on farming?

3. Discuss Masumoto's decision to bring his father home to die. How does he come to this decision? How did you feel when his father wakes up from the coma? During his rehabilitation? As he returns to work at the farm?

4. Throughout the book there are numerous references to "recycling." For example, mementos pass down from generation to generation, and Masumoto uses parts from a "junk pile" to fix his machinery. Which aspects of David Mas Masumoto's family background instilled this virtue of resourcefulness?

6. The book emphasizes many tensions—for example, between technology and hard labor. Think about some other dichotomies. How do these fit into a grander theme?

7. Discuss Masumoto's changing relationship with "weeds." Consider the different ways he uses this term, from the metaphor

about his father's comatose state to the angry letter he addresses to Mr. Johnson about Johnson grass (page 94). Does he view "weeds" as helpful or hurtful? What do they represent to him? To his father?

8. How do you feel about Masumoto's decision to dedicate his life to the family's farm? About Nikiko's decision? Were there any family obligations that changed the trajectory of your life?

9. How do women play a part in this book? Where and how do they fit into the Masumoto family? Into the farming community?

10. Masumoto imparts his wisdom about the economics and politics of farming. Is he optimistic or pessimistic? What did you learn about the farming culture that surprised you?

11. Masumoto describes numerous examples of the unpredictability of nature. What does he learn from situations that are out of his control? Have you had any similar experiences?

12. Are there distinctive generational differences between issei, nisei, and sansei, as Masumoto describes them?

13. Discuss the title of this memoir. What are the implications of the "Last Farmer" as Masumoto sees it?

14. Describe the structure of the book. Was it successful? What did it remind you of? Would you classify the book as more memoir or life-instruction book?

ENHANCE YOUR BOOK CLUB

1. Visit the produce aisle at your local grocery store and buy a selection of peaches you find there (organic and non-organic). Describe the color, skin, texture and taste of the fruits. Do the pits "cling" or are they "freestone"? Consider the differences between the organic and non-organic variations.

2. Draw a family tree and share it with the members of your book group. Is there anything interesting that they might not know about you? Do you have any family histories relating to the immigration experience?

3. Densho is a nonprofit organization that collects oral histories from Japanese Americans who were incarcerated during World War II. Visit their website to learn more about the Japanese American Legacy project: www.densho.org.

4. Learn more about organic farming and the local food movements. Visit websites such as www.slowfoodusa.com or www.organicconsumers.org.

A CONVERSATION WITH DAVID MAS MASUMOTO

1. Did you approach this project more as a personal history or as a life instruction book?

Wisdom began as a personal journey—for weeks following my father's initial stroke in 1997, I kept a daily journal of the challenging situation. I believe it's common during such a crisis to reexamine personal family histories and the connections between family members.

During my father's recovery from the stroke, our relationship changed with a role reversal: I had to teach him how to farm again. Gradually, the lessons I had learned from my father became clearer—along with other discoveries about myself and the person I called my father.

Writing is a wonderful method through which I tackle hard questions and examine transition points. In the case of *Wisdom of the Last Farmer,* writing helped me understand when things will no longer be the same.

What began as a personal journey evolved into broader life lessons I wanted to share. And I have to confess, all this, as my family will attest, makes me kind of moody.

2. Who did you write this book for?

I wrote *Wisdom of the Last Farmer* for those interested in exploring the relationship between fathers and their children and the context of that connection: the places, the family histories, the stories.

For me, our story unfolds on a family farm and through the seem ingly simple, yet complex relationship that is created when you not only work with your father but also must help him heal. The story is nuanced by the fact we farm and grow food. Life is all around us and we must live and work with the rhythms of nature.

I also wrote this for those who want to know more about the story behind their foods—the people and places and the sometimes harsh realities of farming today.

3. Much of the narrative focuses on the decline of your father's health. Was it difficult to put these experiences into words?

Yes. It took years to sort out my feelings while watching this strong man grow older and weaker. The story is complex and does not take place in isolation. Family is always part of this narrative including my wife, children, and my mom. All the while, the farm also continued to change and evolve, along with running a small business in the real world.

A constant question was, how does this all fit together in an honest way? This is not fiction; I can't make up something in order for it to work or make sense. Authenticity is a constant theme in my work.

4. Your passion for harvesting food is apparent in the language you use to describe the color, taste, and feel of fruits. Has writing always come naturally to you or does the subject matter inspire you to write?

Writing is not natural for me. I was a late bloomer in becoming a writer (and hope the best is saved for last!). But I am inspired daily when I head out to work in the fields. I'm always humbled by the joy, beauty, and power of laboring in the earth, growing things and witnessing nature at work. If I can come close to capturing in words some of the drama of our family work, I will consider it a good harvest.

5. You wrote this book as an experienced farmer reflecting on your trials and tribulations. Do you think it would be different to be a young farmer like Nikiko? Are there different challenges today?

Absolutely. Our daughter Nikiko speaks of returning to the farm and taking over. While I will try to pass on my own wisdom, I know the world she faces is changing. Today, people are renewing their relationship with food—it's no longer just a commodity but something more. While some of our work is eternal—peaches need to be irrigated, pruned, and harvested—farming continues to become more complicated, from new regulations and labor issues to marketing challenges and a demand for transparency about agriculture.

Nikiko will also bring her own talents, skills, and perspective to the farm. I expect our farm to change. For example, she had major input in the redesign of our web page and framing our farm with a new public face. (See www.masumoto.com). She claims I can't hide on the farm anymore!

6. Have you had a positive response to your writing from the farming community?

The farming community has been wonderful. I view it as a compliment when many see me as a farmer first and writer second. I remain their neighbor, part of the farm community, and not the voice of an outsider or someone with no intention of staying put. I hope this reflects my honesty in telling not just my story but part of the story of all farm families.

7. Organic food has gained significant attention in recent years. Do you think this increase in awareness has fostered greater appreciation for the work that goes into the products? Does this resonate with the general American public?

Part of the organic agriculture revolution continues to be the relationship people want with their food. They demand to know more. Organic farming and sustainable agriculture strives to reduce the distance between the farm story and consumer interest. It's all part of putting the public frame back into food and agriculture, and I think this is great. People who enjoy our peaches, nectarines, and raisins are not just consumers—I like to think of them as partners. They do have a role in determining how foods are grown.

8. You make references to George Orwell twice in this book.

Is there some connection you have with his work? Has he influenced you? To what extent?
I have long admired Orwell and his ability to tell stories and contextualize meaning, often with a social and political perspective. He was a storyteller and his greatness has made his perspectives universal. I have often reread some of his stories, like *Shooting an Elephant* and of course, was attracted to *Animal Farm* in my youth, believing it was about agriculture. After reading it, I was happy we did not raise pigs on our farm.

9. Have you been inspired by life-instruction books? Which stories or memoirs have had a great impact on you?
Though it was not a memoir, I felt *Grapes of Wrath* was a great story about our valley, our history, and the people that I continue to call my neighbors. The story of struggle and hope bless and haunt me daily when I'm out in the fields.

I also feel many oral histories work like life-instruction books. The many collections by Studs Terkel have influenced my writing as I constantly struggle to find my voice and the collective voice of the places I write about.

I enjoy placed-based books, such as Kathleen Norris's *Dakota* and Richard Hugo's *31 Letters and 13 Dreams,* that are by authors who anchored their work in real people and places.

Finally, I read Zen Buddhist stories and reflect upon their significance for hours while in the fields. Their words linger with me all day as I work.

10. Do you have any plans for another book? If so, what will it be about?
I'm still living with *Wisdom of the Last Farmer* and feel part of "writing a book" is also meeting readers and sharing my voice through readings and presentations. (I list my schedule on our webpage www.masumoto.com.)

Everyday stories continue to intrigue me the most. I'm certain that I'm in the middle of a new book but not exactly sure what the story is—I allow it to grow naturally; sometimes it turns into a weed, other times a flower. As I begin to write, I often find that I'm attracted to the weeds as the most powerful story.

11. Readers might not be familiar with organic farming except for what they read in the pages of your book. Can you suggest any resources for readers who would like to know more?

Read works by Wendell Berry and Michael Pollan.

Explore organizations like Slow Food and the many organic farming groups (such as California Certified Organic Farmers) and sustainable agriculture organizations and their websites (such as the food section of Grist.org).

And the best resources: talking to a farmer at a farmers market, engaging someone in the produce section of a market, or discovering a friend who loves food and exploring the joy of flavor and taste. Perhaps then my stories will have even greater meaning!

BIOGRAPHY & AUTOBIOGRAPHY

Best Environmental Journalism of 2009 from *onEarth* Magazine

"Masumoto passionately engages every fiber of his being in both his work and his writing, bringing the land to life for his readers . . . A philosopher in coveralls and work boots . . . Read slowly and savor."

–*BOOKLIST*

David Mas Masumoto works a family farm, growing organic peaches, nectarines, and grapes. When Masumoto's father has a stroke on the fields of their eighty-acre farm, Masumoto confronts life's big questions: What do his and his father's lives mean? What have they lived and worked for? "A fiercely tender book" (Deborah Madison), *Wisdom of the Last Farmer* "tells the most fascinating kind of story, reminding us that, at its best and most authentic, organic farming requires not only soul, but intimate knowledge of place, a deep grasp of subjects ranging from plant physiology to tractor repair, and unrelenting physical labor" (*onEarth* magazine). In the harvest of his father's wisdom, and his own, gathered from a lifetime of farming and surviving, Mas finds the natural connections between generation and succession and life, death, and renewal. He tells how to tend and make things grow, and how to know when to let nature take over, weaving together stories of life and death to reveal age-old wisdom in what the *The Oregonian* called a "sweet taste of farming, family, loyalty, and dignity." With insights full of beautiful, lyrical descriptions on how to nurture both the tangible and intangible, Masumoto's quiet eloquence reveals how our own destinies are involved in the future of our food, the land, and the farm.

"A graceful meditation on the work of growing food and its meaning across generations. A peach of a book . . . worthy of placement alongside the best of Wendell Berry, Liberty Hyde Bailey and other literary farmers."

–*KIRKUS REVIEWS*

GLENN NAKAMICHI

DAVID MAS MASUMOTO is the award-winning author of *Epitaph for a Peach* and other books, popular columnist, spokesperson for organic farming, and a fellow at The Kellogg Foundation. A third-generation farmer, he grows certified organic peaches, nectarines, and grapes on his family's eighty-acre California farm. He lives in Del Rey, California.

EBOOK EDITION ALSO AVAILABLE

MEET THE AUTHORS, WATCH VIDEOS AND MORE AT
SimonandSchuster.com
THE SOURCE FOR READING GROUPS

COVER DESIGN BY R. GILL • COVER PHOTOGRAPH BY © CHARLES O'REAR/CORBIS

0610

ISBN 978-1-4391-8242-0 **$14.00 U.S./**$18.99 Can.

PRINTED IN THE U.S.A.